Becoming Who You Already Are

A Journey of Self-Discovery and Spiritual Remembering

Kea Rivers

KNOW THYSELF SERIES – BOOK ONE

MIRROR LEAF
PRESS

ISBN: 9781969507007

First Edition

Printed in the United States of America

For permissions or inquiries, contact: riverskea@gmail.com

Contents

A Call to Remember

I grew up in the Christian church. I always felt a calling on my life, and at just fourteen, I chose to be baptized. From that point forward, I served faithfully—anywhere I was needed—and rarely missed a service. Church became my second home. My identity was shaped by what I was taught, what I believed, and how I served.

Years later, during a season of deep ministry work and shortly before publishing my first book, *Mirror Mirror: Seeing Past the Reflection*, I experienced something unexpected—an inner directive. It wasn't audible, but it was unmistakable: *"Sit down and observe."*

That simple instruction stirred something within me. I obeyed, moving from my usual seat to somewhere unfamiliar. As I watched the people around me—singing, praising, lifting hands in worship—I felt something shift. After the message, filled with passion and eloquence, I left wondering what that experience had meant.

Then I heard again, inwardly:

"These people honor me with their lips, but their hearts are far from me."

Even when I wrote about this moment in my first book, I understood it only in part. At the time, I lacked the language to fully express what I felt—but I *knew* it was true. What I would later come to realize is that I had begun a journey: not away from faith, but deeper into it. Not toward rebellion, but toward remembrance.

As a Christian, I wasn't encouraged to *know myself* in the truest sense. I was taught what to believe, not how to *experience* truth. The doctrines I inherited were more about following rules than cultivating inner wisdom.

I was told:
"This is true because we say so."
instead of:
"Discover truth for yourself—through reflection, experience, and resonance."

Mirror Mirror, Seeing Pass the Reflection was born from the desire to see beyond those inherited beliefs. Though shaped by familiar teachings, that book marked the beginning of my unfolding. I wasn't trying to defend what I had been taught. I was reaching for something real—
something that lived beyond dogma.

Now I know: truth isn't a doctrine or a label.
It is an *experience*. A *resonance*. A *remembering*.
We are not merely humans searching for something spiritual.
We are *spiritual beings navigating a human experience*.

Every challenge, every joy, every discomfort is part of the
sacred path back to your true essence, to the core of who you
are beyond the physical form, as a *spiritual being*.

Remembering who you are — *truly* — requires more than belief.
It demands openness. Curiosity. The courage to question
everything you've been taught.

Most people avoid this path not because they lack the ability,
but because it shakes the very foundations of how they've been
taught to exist. It asks them to let go of certainty. To feel. To see.

Self-discovery is exploration.

Self-remembrance is revelation.

Many mystics suggest we aren't learning who we are for the
first time — we're *remembering* what we've forgotten. The divine
spark within you has always been there. Life just covers it up.

If you don't invest in knowing yourself, no one else can do it
for you. No teacher, no book, no sermon can substitute for
your inner knowing.
That is why this book doesn't aim to hand you answers.

It exists as a mirror and a companion—an offering to help you spark your own journey.

You were never meant to fit into a mold.
You were meant to unfold.

If you've read this far, then trust this:
You are already awakening.

This path of self-remembrance asks that you:
- Let go of limiting identities
- Release fear-based conformity
- Listen to the whisper of your intuition
- Honor the experiences that bring you home to yourself

Truth is not inherited. It is revealed—through silence, through resonance, through direct experience.

So, I urge you:
Break free from conditioned roles and beliefs.
Peel back the layers of who you've been told to be.
Listen inward, feel deeply, and remember
who you've always been.

This is not a book of rules.
This is a call to *remember*.

May these words be a gentle spark—
A mirror, a question, a seed—
Planted not to give you the truth,
but to help you remember your own.

Throughout these pages, I'll share pieces of my own journey—
not as a prescription, but as an offering. These reflections are
simply that: stories, insights, and inner shifts that shaped me.
They are not universal truths, and I don't claim to have all the
answers. In fact, I believe a good teacher doesn't pretend to.

A good teacher simply shares what has resonated for them
and trusts you to discern what resonates for you.

I invite you to take what speaks to your spirit and gently leave
what does not. Your path is sacred, unique, and entirely your
own. The most powerful guidance you will ever receive will
come not from my words or anyone else's, but from your own
inner knowing—that deep, quiet wisdom that lives within you.

So as you move through this book, let it be a mirror, not a map.
Let it reflect possibilities, not dictate direction. Trust your
resonance. That's where your truth lives.

This isn't easy. The pursuit of truth may sound noble, even
obvious, but in practice it often asks more than we're prepared
to give.

To truly listen—to ourselves, to others, to the quiet hum

beneath our conditioning—means loosening the grip on what we *think* we know. It means facing the discomfort of not having easy answers, and letting go of the identities we've fused with: Christian, agnostic, activist, skeptic.

These labels can offer belonging, but they can also become armor—protecting us from the tender, unsettling work of unlearning.

The search for truth is not about proving our beliefs right. It begins where certainty ends: in the gentle admission, *"I don't know everything. But I'm willing to listen."*

That kind of listening? It's not passive. It's active. It requires presence. Humility. Sometimes even loss. But what you gain— inner spaciousness, clarity, a relationship with your own aliveness—is worth far more than what you release.

You do not have to become anything. You already are what you seek. — *Mooji*

Before we step into *The Soul Mirror,* I invite you to slow down and be fully present with yourself. This is where the journey inward begins—not with analysis, but with awareness.

The mirror of the soul does not reflect who the world told you to be; it reveals who you have always been beneath the noise. In this space of stillness and reflection, truth begins to rise— not forced but felt.

As we enter this chapter, allow yourself to observe without judgment, to feel without needing to fix, and to remember without fear.

The mirror is not here to shame you—it's here to awaken you.

Chapter 1

The Soul Mirror

The unexamined life is not worth living.
—Socrates

W e begin with a mirror.
But not the kind that hangs on a wall or reflects your outward appearance. The soul mirror is different—it's quieter, subtler, and far more honest. It doesn't capture what's visible, but what's hidden beneath the surface—sometimes buried deep, sometimes yearning to be acknowledged.

When we look into the soul mirror, we aren't seeking to judge or fix. We're simply here to notice. To allow. To witness.

The truth is, you've been gazing into soul mirrors your entire life, whether you recognized it or not. Every experience that stirred you, every relationship that challenged or nurtured you, every recurring habit or pattern—these are all reflections.

Each one reveals something about your inner world: a need, a belief, a fear, a truth.

Your soul is intricately connected to your life. Life is not just the physical world we see, but a spectrum that encompasses your emotions, thoughts, and spirit—your mind, body, and soul. Life is the energy that breathes through you. It is the ever-present mirror reflecting your beliefs and experiences.

If your life mirrors what you believe, what do you see when you look within? And if that reflection is unsettling, how can you change it?

Sometimes, these mirrors are gentle. Other times, they're sharp. But no matter their form, all of them—each one—invite you to know yourself more deeply.

The Gentle Art of Noticing

One of the most profound acts of self-care is simply to notice— not to label, interpret, or fix, but to let the act of noticing be enough. In a world trained to react—always seeking improvement, explanation, or control—the soul mirror asks for none of that. It only asks that you bring your attention, softly and honestly, to what *is*.

In this practice of noticing, you might begin to see:
- Why certain words from a person linger in your mind longer than they should.
- Why a compliment made you feel uneasy rather than uplifted.

- Why the silence in a room can feel either threatening or soothing.

You might notice the sensations in your body—where it tenses, where it softens, where it wants to flee, and where it yearns to stay.

Hidden beliefs and patterns shape your thoughts, emotions, and actions more than you realize. These beliefs often stem from emotional experiences that have been left unexamined. As time passes, the emotions tied to these beliefs can amplify them, making them feel even more entrenched and resistant to change.

When we emotionally invest in a belief, it becomes woven into our identity, and any challenge to it can feel like a threat to our security.

You may begin to notice the tone of your inner voice—when it speaks with kindness, and when it echoes the judgment of an old wound. All of these are reflections. All of them are mirrors. In these moments, you don't need to act. Just let the noticing be enough.

In my own journey, I found that the parts of myself I resisted the most—the emotions I was taught to suppress, the thoughts I harshly judged—were actually gateways.

For a long time, I kept encountering the same frustrating pattern in relationships. I would pour myself out emotionally, energetically, spiritually—until I felt drained, unseen, or quietly resentful.

At first, I framed this overextension as virtuous—selfless, generous, in alignment with what I thought it meant to be "good" or spiritually mature. And when I felt depleted, I would rationalize it with spiritual platitudes: "This is just a test," or "This too shall pass."

But something shifted when I stopped interpreting the experience through familiar beliefs and instead turned inward—not with judgment, but with curiosity.

I asked myself, "What is this discomfort trying to teach me?" It wasn't an immediate answer, but in the stillness that followed, clarity began to rise: beneath my giving, there was a hidden belief—that I had to earn love by proving my worth. That if I gave enough of myself, eventually, I'd feel seen.

This realization unraveled me, but it also began to free me. I realized that much of what I called compassion or humility was actually a mask—rooted in fear, not truth. I wasn't giving from abundance; I was giving from deep inner scarcity.

This insight didn't arrive like a bolt of lightning—it unfolded gently over time. But each time I welcomed it, without resistance, I grew more honest with myself.

I began setting clearer boundaries, questioning old beliefs about worthiness, and allowing real love—love not based on performance—to include me too. Some call this shadow work. I didn't know it by that name at the time.

I simply followed what felt like an inner invitation—a nudge to be honest with myself. Not to judge, not to fix—just to notice and hold space for what I found. And in that space, something softened. Patterns loosened. I began to make choices from a deeper place.

You don't have to follow the same path I did. Your journey will reveal what's needed in its own way. But I offer this as an example: the parts of yourself you fear looking at are often not your enemies—they are the parts of you that need your attention, grace, and love the most.

What I've come to understand is this: the things we most resist—the emotions we suppress, the patterns we judge— are often the gateways to the truest parts of ourselves.

Shadow work is about uncovering those hidden beliefs and patterns. It's the process of confronting the parts of ourselves we've repressed—the fears, the old wounds, the painful truths we try to avoid. It's an alchemical process that transforms the lead of our unconscious shadows into the gold of our authentic selves.

Rooted in both psychology and ancient spiritual traditions, shadow work invites us to explore the unseen parts of ourselves—the aspects of our personality that hide in the shadows of the unconscious. By bringing awareness to these parts, we begin to integrate them and heal, leading to profound personal growth and deeper self-awareness.

Introspection is essential in shadow work. Think of it as shining a light into the dark corners of your psyche, uncovering what's been hidden. It's through introspection that we find the courage to face our shadows, heal old wounds, and ultimately experience emotional freedom.

If anything stirs within you as you read—whether it's a feeling, a memory, or a question—know this: you're not doing anything wrong. You're simply beginning to *see*.

Life as Mirror

There is a quiet power in recognizing that life doesn't just happen around us—it reflects us. Moment by moment, it echoes who we are, what we believe, what we fear, and what we are being called to remember.

When we are guarded, the world feels unwelcoming. When we feel unworthy, even silence can sound like judgment. But when we are open—truly open—life begins to move differently.

Not perfectly. Not always gently. But truthfully.
With alignment, not just outcome.

This is not about blame. It is not about saying you "manifested" your pain or misfortune. Life's hardships are real, and sometimes brutally unfair. But even in their difficulty, they carry messages — not of shame, but of awareness.

What shows up is not always what we want, but often what we are ready — at some level — to *see*. And what you are ready to see is sacred.

Everything in our experience carries a reflection: a person who challenges your peace may be revealing a boundary you haven't yet honored. A situation that exhausts you may be pointing to the story you're still carrying about your worth. The people who uplift you are often mirroring the beauty you've forgotten to claim as your own.

Even stillness reflects: whether we fear it, crave it, or resist it — it reveals something true.

To view life as a mirror is not to spiritualize harm or bypass pain. It is to hold a deeper posture of awareness — one that sees very experience as part of a larger unfolding. A sacred invitation to tend inwardly, not just react outwardly.

This is what it means to reclaim spiritual responsibility. Not the kind that says, "it's all your fault," but the kind that says: *you have agency in how you meet this moment.*

When you tend to the inner landscape, you shift how the outer world feels—not because it changes instantly, but because *you* begin seeing differently.

The mirror does not shame. It does not punish. It simply reveals. And in that revealing, it offers a choice: to notice, to honor, and—when you are ready—to begin again.

So the next time life feels sharp or uncertain, pause. Instead of asking *"Why is this happening to me?"* try asking:
"What is this showing me about what I still carry?"
"What part of me is seeking to be healed, seen, or set free?"

The mirror doesn't lie. But it also doesn't condemn.
It simply waits, patiently, for you to look—
and to recognize yourself with new eyes.

Reflection Is Not Fixing

Reflection often arrives disguised—as a difficult conversation, an unexpected emotion, a repeated experience. These moments, and the people within them, can act as mirrors, revealing something deeper within us.

But contrary to what we've been taught, reflection doesn't demand that we correct or improve ourselves on the spot. It doesn't exist to shame or rush us—it exists to show us something we might have overlooked.

Whether the mirror comes in the form of your own thoughts or through life's interactions, its purpose is not to criticize. Its gift is clarity. To reflect is not to fix, but to witness.

The mirror does not demand transformation.
It doesn't whisper, *"Be better."*
It simply offers, *"Here you are."*

This chapter is not a call to action. It's a call to presence.
To sit beside yourself—perhaps for the first time in a long while—and gently say:
I see you.

No pressure. No timeline. Just honest, compassionate witnessing.

In a world driven by self-improvement, we are conditioned to treat discomfort as a flaw, to believe that anything unresolved within us must be immediately managed, corrected, or erased. But true reflection doesn't ask for fixing. It asks for presence.

When you look in a mirror, it does not accuse. It does not label your face or feelings as wrong. It simply reflects what is—with clarity, not judgment. And in the same way, life—through quiet moments, relationships, or emotions—mirrors back your inner world. Not to shame you into change, but to invite awareness.

Reflection is not a performance.
It's not about proving you're evolving.
It's about being with what arises, as it is.

Fixing often springs from shame—the belief that something in you is broken, unworthy, or too much.

Reflection, by contrast, is rooted in love.
It says:
This is part of me.
This, too, deserves space.
This, too, belongs.

When we rush to solve what we find, we miss the medicine. We start editing ourselves into worthiness, instead of remembering that our worth was never in question. We begin managing ourselves like problems, rather than honoring ourselves as sacred mysteries.

To reflect is to return—to your essence, not your performance.
It is to look in the soul's mirror and say:
I am willing to see.
Not to fix. Not to flee.
But to witness, listen, and love what surfaces.

Healing comes from this space.
Not through force, but through permission.
Not by rushing forward, but by gently turning inward.

So when the mirror reveals something raw or unfamiliar,
don't ask, *"What's wrong with me?"*
Ask:
"What is this showing me?"
"What part of me is asking to be held with compassion?"

Reflection is how we begin to walk ourselves home.
Not to become someone new—but to remember who we
already are, beneath the layers.

Two of the ways I engage in this process of remembering are
through journaling and meditation. Journaling has given me a
space to name my emotions, notice patterns, and uncover
hidden beliefs with honesty and compassion. Meditation—still
a practice I'm learning to trust—offers another doorway into
presence and deeper awareness. It has allowed me to slow
down enough to feel what I once avoided, and to sit with what
surfaces without running from it.

These practices weren't about fixing myself. They were about
befriending myself. And that shift—*from self-improvement to
self-acceptance*—changed everything.

What You See Is Not All There Is

A mirror can show us what is visible—but it can also invite us into what is not. When we look into life as a mirror, we begin to sense that appearances are only part of the story. Beneath the surface of every moment, every emotion, and every interaction, something deeper is being revealed—not to judge us, but to awaken us.

Mirrors have long held power—both literal and symbolic. They reflect surfaces, yes—but they also stir something deeper. They hint at the unseen.

Now imagine your soul as a mirror.
Not made of glass, but of presence.
It doesn't just reflect the world around you—
it reflects the truth within you.

At first, what you see might be the most obvious or noisy: fear, judgment, grief, defensiveness. These tend to rise first. They live closer to the surface because they've learned to shout the loudest.

But beneath them—beneath the layers shaped by survival, expectation, and illusion—live quieter truths.

Tenderness. Longing. A soft ache to be seen.
A voice that was silenced.
A memory still waiting to be honored.

A sacred part of you, asking not to be fixed—but to be felt.

These truths do not demand. They wait.
They emerge when you are safe enough,
still enough, ready enough.

So you don't have to chase them.
You don't have to dig or force anything to rise.
Let your reflection come to you.

Life has a way of holding up soul mirrors when we need them
most. They don't always come in rituals or retreats.
Sometimes they appear in the messy middle of everyday life:
A relationship that tests your boundaries.
A familiar emotional wave that arrives out of nowhere.
A repeated pattern you swore you'd outgrown.

These moments are not failures.
They are invitations.

The soul mirror doesn't scold.
It doesn't say *"You're not healed enough."*
It says, *"Here's something you're ready to see."*

In my own journey, I once mistook reflection for inadequacy.
If something triggered me, I thought it meant I wasn't doing
enough inner work—or worse, that I was moving backwards.
But I've come to understand: reflection is not punishment. It's
presence. It's not an indictment. It's an opening.

A soft but unmistakable nudge from the universe saying,
**Come back. Be here. With yourself. With your truth.
With what was forgotten.**

You don't have to force these openings.
You don't have to hunt for mirrors.
They will find you—at the right time, in the right form.
A conversation. A conflict. A sudden tenderness.
And when they do, you'll know.
Because something in you will pause.
Something in you will whisper,
This matters. Pay attention.

These reflections don't define you.
They reveal you.
And what they reveal isn't flaw—it's fullness.

Let it come.
Let it unfold in its own rhythm.
Let it speak when it's ready.

Because what you see is not all there is.
There is more.
And it's been waiting for you all along.

This Is the Beginning

There is nothing to master here.
No checklist to complete.

No gold star for doing it "right."

The mirror is already present.
It lives in your daily life—in your conversations, your
emotions, your stillness, and your discomfort.
This chapter is simply an invitation to begin *noticing*.

You might leave these pages and feel your day differently.
You might speak with someone and, suddenly, something
clicks: *this moment is a mirror.*

You might feel irritation and pause—not to judge, but to ask:
"What is being shown to me here?"
You might feel peace and wonder:
"Is this what wholeness looks like reflected back to me?"

These are not signs that you've done something "right."
They are signs that you are *seeing* with new eyes.
This is where transformation begins.
Not in striving to become someone else,
but in recognizing who you already are—
beneath the noise, beyond the roles.

Self-examination of the soul is not a task.
It is a return.
A sacred pause to check in with your inner being.
The soul is your essence—your undying, unedited self.
It carries your longings, your joys, your wounds,
and your wisdom.

It is not here to be fixed.
It is here to be remembered.

You are not being asked to rush.
You are not being asked to solve.
Only to be with what has stirred.
To witness, with compassion, whatever rises.
To listen with gentleness, even if nothing makes sense yet.

The mirror doesn't change the world around you.
It changes the *way* you see it.
And in time, as your awareness deepens, the mirror becomes clearer—polished by presence, softened by love.

Eventually, it reflects something more than just your surface self. It reflects the Divine.
The part of you that was never lost.
The part of you that knows.

That, too, is sacred.

The soul mirror is not made of glass—it is made of awareness. Every emotion, every relationship, every moment of resistance or relief, can show you something about your inner world.

The work is not to fix the reflection.
The work is to honor it.

So I invite you to begin.

Not with effort.
But with willingness.

What do you see when you look into your life as a mirror?

Let that question linger.
Let it open something new.
Let it guide you—not toward perfection,
but toward presence.

This is not the end.
This is the beginning.

Chapter 2

The Body as Oracle

The body says what words cannot.
—Martha Graham

Your body has been speaking in sacred whispers all along. We are often taught to seek wisdom outside ourselves—through doctrines, experts, systems. But nestled closer than any external guide is a profound source of truth: your body. Not the body as object, task, or image—but as a living oracle, a vessel of spirit, a keeper of the unseen.

Before your mind learned words, your body was already listening, already remembering. Every moment of joy, every wound, every experience of safety or violation has left its imprint—not only in muscle and breath, but in the energy that animates you.

Your body speaks in sensation, in rhythm, in stillness and tremble. In presence. It holds frequencies your mind may not yet understand. It remembers what you've forgotten, and reveals truths too deep for language. It is not separate from your spirit—it is an expression of it. A compass. A sanctuary. A mirror.

Your body is the living temple of your soul's journey.

To return to it is not a trend, nor an obligation. It is a sacred choice. A re-alignment with the intelligence that has always been within you.

This chapter is not here to tell you what you must feel or believe. It is a gentle invitation—to listen more deeply.
To trust your own resonance.
To choose what feels true, and
to release what does not.

There is no one path. Only the one that calls to you.

Learning the Language of Sensation

You may begin to notice a quiet shift—a soft pull inward,
a sense that knowing doesn't always arrive through thought.
What if insight could come not as an answer, but as a feeling?
What if the wisdom you seek has been speaking all along—
in the hush beneath the noise, in the pulse beneath the story?

This isn't about abandoning the mind.
It's about welcoming another voice:
the one that speaks through sensation, rhythm, resonance.

You are invited to listen—
not to force understanding,
but to become available to it.

Begin simply. Begin gently.

The mind is quick—it races to narrate, explain, assess. It
reaches outward for answers, weaving meaning from thought.
But the body moves in another rhythm. Slower. Truer.
It doesn't speak in concepts or conclusions—
it speaks in energy, in resonance, in felt knowing.

While the mind may seek logic, the body reveals alignment.
It speaks in subtle signs: a quickening heartbeat, a drop in your
belly, a softening of your jaw, a sudden stillness.

These are not random reactions. They are messages.
Echoes from the soul through the medium of form.

This wisdom is not loud, but it is steady. And it rarely lies.

Notice what arises in your body when you move through the
world—not just what you think, but what you *feel*. In certain
rooms. With certain people. After a conversation.
Beneath fluorescent lights. In the hush of trees.

Do you expand or contract? Does your breath flow or catch?
Does your skin tingle, or your chest grow heavy?

These are not symptoms to be dismissed.
They are signals.
Invitations.

This *is* the language of your oracle.
This *is* truth, before the mind has time to edit.

As you listen more deeply, you may begin to see patterns:
- A flutter in your chest before something beautiful unfolds.
- Your jaw tightening before your thoughts catch up to a boundary being crossed.
- Warmth spreading when you're in alignment, resonance, truth.
- Fatigue where your energy no longer belongs.
- A shiver when words land directly in your soul.

This is not fantasy.
This is not performance.
This is embodiment.
This is sacred memory stirring in the flesh.

The body offers you presence—not performance.
Connection—not conditioning.
It does not ask you to conform; it asks you to *feel*.

Learning to listen is not about perfection. It's about *presence*.
About honoring the living instrument you've always carried.

Let this be a return—not to doctrine, but to *direct knowing*.
Not to external truth, but to the voice of the soul,
housed in tissue, tremor, and tenderness.

You are not broken for not knowing how to hear it yet.
You are simply remembering a language you were never
meant to forget.

Reclaiming the Wisdom Within

The journey inward is not about adding more—it's about
listening more deeply. Beneath the noise of external opinions
and internal overthinking lives a quiet wisdom that has always
been with you. It does not clamor for attention. It waits—
patiently—for you to turn toward it and remember.

Within each of us lives a chorus of voices. Some arise from the
ego—shaped by fear, control, and past survival. Others rise
from deeper ground: the voice of the body as oracle.

This voice does not argue, persuade, or perform.
It simply waits—for you to feel.

The ego often speaks first. And loudest. It draws from the
familiar: old wounds, learned defenses, inherited beliefs.

Its messages can feel urgent, even authoritative—
because they once kept you safe.
But safety and truth are not always the same.

By contrast, the body's oracle speaks in quieter ways. It does
not demand. It does not threaten. It speaks through sensation,
through pause, through the softening or clenching of your

muscles, the rhythm of your breath, the expansion or contraction in your chest.

It is the voice of *now*, not the echo of what once was.
The ego seeks to *control* life.
The body reveals where life is already *in motion*.

Neither voice is "wrong." Both have served a purpose.
But the sacred task is in learning to discern—
not from a place of judgment, but from presence.

To notice:
- What tightens you vs. what opens you.
- What feels forced vs. what feels true.
- What is rooted in fear vs. what is grounded in resonance.

The ego wants to be the oracle of your life: the final word, the keeper of rules, the judge of worthiness. It speaks with certainty, even when its certainty is born of fear.

The body, meanwhile, does not seek to convince. It simply *reflects* what is.

To let the body lead is not to reject thought, but to restore balance. To bring the sacred back into your sensing. To remember that truth isn't always logical—but it is always felt.

Many of us were taught to override the body. To dismiss feeling as weakness. To silence sensation. To trust only the intellect. But there is another way. A more ancient way.

When we stop trying to fix or force—and instead pause to *feel*—we enter a deeper conversation.
One that includes the mind but does not worship it.
One that honors the wisdom of the whole self—
mind, body, spirit.

To reclaim this wisdom is not rebellion. It is reunion.

What Does Safety Feel Like?

This is not a question for the mind to solve, but for the body to answer. What does safety *feel* like—not as a concept, not as an appearance, but as a living experience in your body?

Not what *should* feel safe.
Not what others *say* is safe.
But what your being recognizes as safety in its own sacred language.

You may notice:
- A softening in your chest
- A breath that arrives without effort
- A loosening in your belly
- A gentle spaciousness behind your eyes
- A sense that you can *exist* without performing

These are not just physical responses—they are soul signals. Signs that your body recognizes presence, connection, and rest.

Your body knows when it is welcome.
It knows when it is held.
And just as it knows safety, it knows when something is not aligned—even when the mind offers reasons to stay.
Even when logic whispers "You're overreacting."
Even when appearances suggest otherwise.

The mind is fast. It sorts and strategizes. It's skilled in storytelling, in making sense of things. But sensing is not the mind's domain.

The body speaks in subtler ways—
a flutter in the gut,
a held breath,
a pulse of warmth,
a rising tension in the jaw.

It does not accuse.
It does not negotiate.
It simply *responds.*

This wisdom is ancient—older than language, deeper than thought. It lives in fascia and frequency, in intuition and instinct. Yet, many of us were taught to override it.
To dismiss the whispers. To numb the ache.
To mistrust the very guidance that was always with us.

Your body has never stopped speaking.
Even in silence, it has been waiting—for you to ask, to feel,
to return.

So ask gently, without pressure or expectation:
What does safety feel like *for me*—right now, in this breath?

Let this be your compass.
Let this be your truth.

Personal Reflection:
When My Body Told Me the Truth

There was a time when I was very close to a family member that I love deeply. It caught me off guard—suddenly, even the most harmless things I said, like asking "What time is it?" seemed to stir tension I didn't understand. At first, I brushed it off. I told myself they were going through something, and because we were so close, maybe they were just taking it out on me.

But even then, my body didn't feel at ease. There was a tightness I couldn't name. A quiet discomfort I tried to ignore to "keep the peace."

Then came the day that was meant to celebrate me—a moment when I should have felt safe, seen, and honored. But instead, everything was turned upside down.

This same family member that I love deeply made it memorable in all the wrong ways. That was the moment I could no longer explain away the feeling in my body.

I asked them to leave. I blocked contact—not to punish, but to protect. To protect my peace. To protect the soft space I'm learning to build inside.

That decision didn't come from logic alone. It came from my body. From the place inside me that recognized what safety *doesn't* feel like. Listening to my body helped me make a loving boundary.

This, too, is what safety feels like.

In learning to honor the truth in my body, I wasn't turning away from love—I was turning toward a deeper one.
One that begins with me.

Letting the Body Speak

Wisdom does not always arrive as thought. Sometimes it emerges as sensation, stillness, or subtle knowing. The body remembers what the mind forgets. It carries truths too sacred for language—truths that surface not through effort, but through presence.

Today, you are invited to let your body speak—
not with words, but with presence.

Not to interrogate.
Not to critique.

But to soften into communion and simply ask:
"What are you holding?"
"What are you ready to share?"
"What truth lives here, just beneath the surface?"

Let it be simple. Let it be slow.

You might:
- Lie on the ground and let gravity hold you.
- Walk in silence, barefoot if you can, feeling the rhythm of your steps.
- Rest your hand on your heart or belly and listen — not for answers, but for awareness.
- Move in a way that feels natural, unplanned, uncensored. Let the body guide.

This is not about performance.
This is about relationship.
Your body has always longed for a relationship with *you*.

The mind races forward and back, looping through time, story, expectation.

But the body only lives *here.*
In this breath.

This pulse.
This moment.
It doesn't bargain.
It doesn't argue.
It doesn't pretend.

It simply reveals—
when you're nearing your edge,
when you're carrying more than you've named,
when your soul craves stillness or movement, release or rest.

The body is not a machine to manage. It is a temple of truth.
A companion. A compass. A vessel for the sacred.

It speaks not to correct you, but to connect you.
Not to demand more, but to offer grace.

When you let the body lead, you step out of the noise and into
now. And *now* is the portal—to healing, to wholeness,
to remembering who you truly are.

You Get to Choose

There is a quiet power in remembering that the answers you
seek are not out there—they live within. Amid all the noise,
the advice, the expectations, your inner knowing remains. Not
demanding, but steady. Not loud, but true.

The journey back to yourself is not about adopting someone

else's map. It's about learning to trust the compass already inside you.

A Return to Inner Sovereignty
Let this be your invitation —
not to follow, but to *feel.*
Not to be told, but to *remember.*

Some truths rise like warmth in the belly.
Some echo in the throat, the chest, the spine.
Some come in dreams, in stillness, in tears you didn't expect.
Some speak through exhaustion, resistance, or sudden release.
Your body carries its own sacred dialect.
And only *you* can translate it.

There is no single path. No formula.
No one ritual or rhythm meant for every soul.
What grounds one person might unmoor another.
What felt like truth yesterday may move in a new direction tomorrow.

This isn't failure or confusion.
This is *aliveness.* This is *wisdom that breathes.*
The invitation is not to find a fixed answer,
but to reclaim your right to *choose.*

You get to choose which voice you trust.
You get to choose when to speak, when to rest, when to say

31

no. You get to choose what feels like nourishment, what feels like misalignment, what feels like *truth—for you.*

The body doesn't always speak in sentences.
But it remembers.

It knows the shape of "yes."
It recognizes the cost of self-abandonment.
And it will speak—through breath, through ache, through knowing—until you choose to listen.

No external voice can make that choice for you.
Not mine.
Not anyone's.

I am not here to chart your path, but to hold a lantern while you remember: your compass never stopped working.
It was just waiting for you to trust it again.

If you've spent a lifetime being told who to be, how to feel, or what to believe—know this chapter holds no map.
Because *you are the map.*

This is the key it places in your palm:
You get to choose.

Perhaps, that is the most sacred truth of all.

The Oracle Is Alive

The wisdom you seek is not locked in doctrine or distant realms—it lives within you. Not as static knowledge, but as a living, breathing presence.

Your body is not separate from truth; it is one of its oldest messengers.

This is the invitation: to return to your own inner oracle— not once, but continually. To listen, not for answers alone, but for relationship.

This is not a chapter to complete.
It is a place to return to—again and again.
Because each time you meet your body,
it may speak in a new voice.

Some days, it will whisper.
Other days, it may thunder.
But always—it speaks.

The question is not, *"Can I hear it?"*
The deeper question is, *"Am I willing to listen—without rushing to fix, explain, or override?"*

We often imagine self-knowing as a purely mental or spiritual pursuit. But the body is where truth lands.
It's where knowing becomes lived.

You may *believe* you've forgiven —
yet feel your chest tighten at the sound of their name.
You may *know* you're safe —
yet still sense your body brace when old patterns arise.
This is not contradiction.
This is information.
This is the body inviting you into deeper integration.

Let this not be a lesson in mastery —
but in presence.
Let it be an invitation to pause,
to ask with tenderness,
to listen with care.

Let the oracle speak.
Let yourself receive.
And trust: what arises in this moment is not a mistake.
It's what you're meant to notice now.

Letting your body be the oracle is not about idolizing form.
It's about honoring the sacredness of *being here,*
in this vessel, in this breath.

It's the quiet knowing that says:
*"My truth isn't just an idea. It lives in my chest, in my spine,
in the places that ache and soften."*

Your body is not a puzzle to solve.

Not a project to perfect.
It is a compass. A guide.

A living oracle with its own ancient language.
And it's been speaking to you all along.

Chapter 3

Mirrors in the World

Everyone comes into our lives to mirror back to us
some part of ourselves we cannot or will not see.
—Iyanla Vanzant

We are never just seeing others—we are always, in some way, seeing ourselves. This is one of the tender and sometimes uncomfortable truths on the path of remembering who we are. The world, in all its beauty, chaos, and complexity, does not simply exist *out there*—it moves with us, speaks to us, and mirrors us. People, relationships, fleeting interactions, even moments that stir irritation or awe, often carry reflections of what we have yet to fully meet, love, or integrate within ourselves.

This isn't simply poetic language. It is energetic reality. When something moves you—whether it lifts you or unsettles you—you are being invited into deeper relationship with a part of yourself.

The external becomes a spark, not a sentence.
A mirror, not a measure.

Every soul you cross paths with carries a reflection. Not a literal mirror, but an energetic one. Some offer glimpses of your light—your capacity for joy, courage, compassion, or truth. Others reveal your shadows—places where fear, grief, or old wounds still speak louder than love.

Sometimes the mirror feels gentle: a stranger's kindness softens you, a friend's wisdom resonates deep in your spirit, someone's boldness reminds you of a strength you've tucked away. Other times, the reflection comes with friction: a comment leaves you stung, a tone throws you off balance, a family member's choices press against everything you've worked so hard to heal.

These moments are not punishments—they are teachers. Not because they are "right," but because they reveal where your soul is asking for your attention, your care, and your truth.

This chapter is about those mirrors.

It is about learning to notice—not just what others are doing— but what you are feeling in their presence. It's about learning to pause and ask:
"Why does this moment linger in me?"
"What is being stirred? What story is being activated?"
"What is this showing me about how I see myself?"

To know thyself is to meet the world as a reflection, not a battlefield. It is to shift from blame to self-inquiry.

From reactivity to remembrance.

Strong emotional responses are often trailheads—signposts pointing not just to what happened *out there*, but to what still longs to be seen, honored, or reclaimed *within*.

Sometimes what we judge in others mirrors the places where we still carry judgment toward ourselves. Sometimes what we admire in others is a part of us quietly asking to be lived out loud. Sometimes what we allow or endure reflects the old stories that taught us to betray our own boundaries or silence our truth.

The path to truth is not a rigid destination. It begins with humility. With a willingness to be honest. With the courage to admit: *"Maybe I don't yet know myself as deeply as I desire to. But I'm willing to look. I'm willing to listen."*

This chapter does not ask you to shame yourself for your reactions. It asks you to hold them gently. To sit with what unsettles you—not always with the other person, but with your own heart. With compassion. With curiosity. With the kind of loving honesty that heals.

Ask:
"What part of me is being mirrored here?"
"What story, what pattern, what longing or wound is asking to be acknowledged?"

"What truth within me is this moment trying to awaken?"

So as you journey through this book, may you hold it as a mirror, not a rulebook. Let it reflect possibilities, not dictate direction. Trust what stirs you. Trust what resonates. Trust what feels like home in your body and spirit.

That's where your truth lives.

Let this chapter be a gentle reminder of something sacred: The world is not just happening to you. It's revealing you—moment by moment, reflection by reflection—so that you may return home to yourself.

The Reflective Principle

Pay attention to the people who stir something in you—especially the ones who evoke strong emotion. Notice what you find yourself resisting, admiring, envying, or judging. These responses are not random. They are energetic signals—breadcrumbs guiding you inward.

Ask, gently:
"Is there something in this person that reflects a part of me I've hidden, disowned, or not yet allowed to come fully alive?"

"Do I see in them a version of myself I've longed to express but haven't given myself permission to become?"

"Is this discomfort pointing to a boundary, a belief, or a fear that's ready to be seen?"

This is not to say that others' behaviors are your responsibility, or that every reaction is a projection. The Reflective Principle isn't about blame—it's about awareness.

It invites you to explore: *What is this interaction revealing about my relationship with myself?*

There's a quiet truth living in every encounter: the people we meet often reflect something back to us. Not always clearly. Not always kindly. But consistently.

Some mirrors are warm. You meet someone, and something in you exhales. You feel seen, inspired, understood. Their presence reminds you of your own light, your own capacity, your own forgotten dreams.

Other mirrors are sharper. A tone unsettles you. A behavior activates an old wound. You feel judgment rising, or a familiar ache you can't quite name. These moments can be painful, but they are also potent. They show you where healing is still unfolding.

This is the essence of the Reflective Principle:
What you notice *out there* often carries a message about what is alive *in here*—within you.

When you're deeply affected by someone, pause and gently inquire:

"What part of me is reacting right now?"

"Is this mirroring something I haven't yet made peace with—or a part of me that's longing to be honored?"

"Is this discomfort asking me to speak up, set a boundary, or soften something I've held too tightly?"

Equally, when you feel awe or resonance in someone's presence, that, too, is meaningful. It may be a reflection of your emerging self—your readiness to step into something fuller, freer, more true.

Looking into these mirrors isn't always easy. Some reflections feel distorted, confusing, even painful. But the purpose of the mirror is not to punish—it's to reveal. And once something is seen with compassion, it can be transformed.

This doesn't mean you spiritualize harm or excuse mistreatment. Not every mirror is meant to be lingered in. Sometimes, the reflection is clear because you've outgrown the pattern it
reveals. Sometimes, the lesson is in the leaving.

The Reflective Principle asks not for self-blame, but for self-inquiry. It invites you to ask:

"What is this showing me about who I've been — and who I'm becoming?"

"What truth is this experience uncovering?"

"What part of me is being asked to awaken, to protect, or to love more fully?"

In this way, every interaction — pleasant or painful — becomes sacred. Not because it's easy, but because it holds potential. It carries information about your alignment, your boundaries, your becoming.

Ultimately, to see yourself through the eyes of others is not to lose yourself. It is to gather the scattered pieces. To bring home what's been exiled. To remember your wholeness.

Let the world be your mirror.
Not to criticize the reflection —
But to witness the truth of who you are,
and who you are still unfolding into.

Applying the Reflective Principle:
A Personal Story

At one point in my life, I found myself deeply triggered by the emotional dynamics between my mother and my brother. I was serving as my mother's caregiver — she was 84 at the time, facing multiple medical challenges — and I was doing my best to offer her the compassionate support she deserved. Yet beneath that commitment was a layered and exhausting emotional landscape, woven with love, duty, heartbreak, and, at times, quiet resentment.

My mother has long maintained a co-dependent relationship with my brother, who struggles with drug addiction. Watching her repeatedly rescue him, shield him from consequences, and sacrifice her own well-being became increasingly painful. And then, one day, it hit me: I wasn't just observing the pattern— I was entangled in it.

Using the Reflective Principle, I paused to ask: *What in them is mirroring something I've disowned or not fully honored in myself?*

My mother became a mirror for my own inner rescuer.
Just as she tried to save my brother, I was trying to save her— from him. I wanted her to wake up, to break the cycle, to choose herself. But she wouldn't—or perhaps couldn't— and that broke my heart.

In my effort to rescue her, I was unknowingly reenacting the same exhausting role, believing that if I just loved enough, tried hard enough, or explained it clearly enough, I could change the outcome.

My brother was the mirror that revealed my mother.
Over time, I began to see that it was through my brother that my mother's pattern came into focus. The way he took her love

and support for granted mirrored something deeper—
something I hadn't fully named. He acted as if she owed him
simply because he was her son.

And through that lens, I began to realize: she was doing the
same with me. Expecting my care, my presence, my emotional
labor, as if it were a debt I owed simply because I'm her
daughter.

It was a painful realization—a reflection of a generational
pattern of silent obligation, dressed up as love. And I was in the
middle of it all—shouldering the emotional weight of two
people who believed love meant being owed.

I was carrying the weight of both their expectations, while the
quiet needs of my own soul went unseen—even by me.

These realizations were painful—but profoundly liberating.

I came to see that love and enabling are not the same. That
helping someone doesn't mean saving them. And that staying
aligned with my peace would sometimes require saying no—
even to those I love.

So I began to set boundaries. Clear, calm, compassionate—but
firm.

- With my mother, I refused to participate in enabling

behavior. I would no longer help facilitate any form of support that allowed my brother to avoid accountability.

- With my brother, I limited our contact and made it clear that, as my mother's Power of Attorney, I would not allow her limited fixed income to be used to fund his habits or shield him from the natural consequences of his choices.

These decisions weren't easy. My mother still gets emotional and, at times, tries to test those limits. But I stay grounded in my reasons—because I know they are rooted not in punishment, but in protection.

My peace is non-negotiable.

Caring for others doesn't mean abandoning yourself.
Love doesn't mean surrendering your sanity.
Boundaries are not rejection—they are a form of respect.

For my own well-being, I turned to journaling, meditation, and movement—biking, walking, stretching. These practices didn't just help me manage stress; they helped me return to myself. To the quiet space where my inner voice still speaks.

This part of the journey taught me that the Reflective Principle isn't just about awareness—it's about *alignment*. It's about listening to what life is showing you through others, and then making the choices that restore your integrity.

Projection and Resonance

When the world becomes a mirror, not everything it shows is literal. Sometimes what unsettles us in others is a reflection of what we've yet to tend within. Sometimes what draws us in is the echo of a truth we're just beginning to reclaim.

These moments—whether charged or magnetic—
aren't random. They are invitations.
To pause.
To listen.
To wonder: *What in me is being shown here?*

There are times when what we see in others isn't really about them—it's about us. We project what we haven't yet made peace with. We resonate with what we're just beginning to remember. Both experiences are part of the same sacred dance.

You may find yourself stirred by a friend's courage—and realize it touches a longing within you to live more boldly.
Or perhaps a colleague's arrogance unsettles you—not because they're wrong, but because it brushes up against your own complicated relationship with confidence.
A stranger's warmth might move you, not only for its beauty, but because it reflects a tenderness you've tucked away.

These are not judgments. They're reflections—quiet signals from the deeper self. When seen with curiosity instead of critique, they become invitations. Doorways into self-awareness. Portals back to wholeness.

We are always in relationship: With others. With our history. With the parts of ourselves we've embraced—and the parts we've exiled. And often, without even realizing it, we place those inner parts *onto* others. We turn people into characters in our inner drama—heroes, threats, teachers, reminders.

This is projection.

Projection happens when we unconsciously assign others a role in our story.

A sharp comment might pierce deeper than expected— not because of its content, but because of what it activates. A loved one's silence might feel like rejection—not because they're withdrawing, but because an old wound is echoing. Someone else's success might stir your insecurity. Their pain might awaken your guilt. It's not always about them. Often, it's about what they awaken in *you*.

Projection isn't wrong—it's just unexamined. And when left unseen, it blurs the boundary between what is *yours* and what is *theirs*.

Others are responsible for their behavior, yes. But the charge you feel—the heat, the ache, the tightness—that's your mirror calling you inward.

On the other side of projection lives something just as powerful: **resonance**.

Resonance is when something in the outer world harmonizes with an inner truth. It's that moment when someone speaks and your whole being quietly says, *yes*.

Not because their voice is louder, but because their truth sounds like your own.

It's the flicker of recognition when you see someone living with grace, power, or presence—and a whisper rises: *That's me too. I remember now.*

If projection surfaces what we haven't yet healed, resonance reveals what we're ready to reclaim.
Not because we were ashamed. But because we were afraid.
Afraid of being too much.
Afraid of being misunderstood.
Afraid of stepping into the very essence we were born to embody.

Both projection and resonance are teachers.
Both point the way home.
One asks: *What am I hiding from?*
The other whispers: *What part of me is longing to be expressed?*

The people who challenge us and the ones who move us are often holding the same mirror—just tilted at different angles.

Each offers a gift.

If we can pause, breathe, and stay curious...
If we can hold back the impulse to fix, to judge, to flee...
We might hear something deeper rise beneath the surface:

> *"This isn't about them. It's about you. Pay attention."*

Discomfort as Teacher

Discomfort rarely feels welcome. But more often than not, it's the most honest teacher we'll ever have. Sometimes it shows up in a clear mirror—sharp and unmistakable. Other times, the mirror is smudged, distorted, hard to decipher.

But whether it's glaring or subtle, discomfort is almost always a sign: *There's something here worth paying attention to.*

When you feel a sudden emotional spike—a tightening in the chest, a flush of anger, a defensive urge—it helps to pause and ask:
"What part of me is reacting right now?"
"Is this a wound being touched?"
"What am I afraid someone might see in me?"
"What do I secretly wish I could embody more freely?"

The mirror isn't here to judge. It's here to reflect.
You are allowed to look. You are allowed to feel.
And you are allowed to choose what this reflection means for
you.

Discomfort is often the first knock when a mirror appears.
It doesn't arrive wrapped in clarity or softness.
It comes as heat in the face. A snap in your voice.
A wave of shame you didn't expect.

It rarely whispers—it jolts.
But that doesn't mean it's cruel.
It means it's *trying* to be heard.

We live in a culture conditioned to avoid discomfort at all
costs. We push it away, numb it, explain it, project it.
But discomfort doesn't come to punish—it comes to point.
It's not always a sign that something's wrong.
Sometimes, it's a sign that something inside is waking up.

When someone triggers you, pause.
Instead of asking, "What's wrong with *them*?" try:
"What is this feeling showing me about myself?"

Maybe they mirror back a boundary you've never felt safe
enforcing. Maybe they awaken an old version of you that
once kept you safe—but now keeps you small. Maybe they stir
the ache of being unseen, unheard, unacknowledged.

Discomfort is a mirror that doesn't flatter.
But it does tell the truth.

Sometimes, the person who makes your skin crawl is reflecting a part of you that you've exiled. Sometimes, the one who always needs saving is reminding you of the identity you're finally ready to release—the fixer, the martyr, the one who never stops giving. Sometimes, the loud or needy or selfish one is simply waking up the part of you that's tired of being quiet, invisible, contained.

The goal is not to shame yourself for being triggered.
The goal is to become *curious* about the trigger.
To sit with the discomfort long enough to ask:
"Where have I felt this before?"
"What story am I telling myself right now?"
"What part of me is being stirred, silenced, or forgotten?"

Discomfort isn't your enemy—it's your invitation.
To revisit the patterns you've inherited.
To meet the wounds you've avoided.
To remember the truths you've buried beneath survival.

And here's the grace: once discomfort teaches what it came to teach, it often softens. It no longer needs to scream.
The mirror that once stung becomes a window—
into a fuller, truer version of you.

I remember a time this lesson hit home. Someone in my family—someone I love deeply—repeatedly disrespected and humiliated me. The pain reached a breaking point.

It wasn't just uncomfortable—it was intolerable. Their behavior crossed a line so sharp, I had to act. I chose to set firm boundaries, even blocking contact to protect my peace.

This wasn't an easy decision. It hurt deeply because love was still present. So was history.

I wrote to them—not to attack, but to share a hope: that maybe one day, if true acknowledgment and change emerged, something could be rebuilt.

That rupture taught me something essential:
Growth means loving yourself enough to step away from what keeps you small, silent, or unseen.

It means understanding that honoring your well-being isn't selfish—it's sacred.

Discomfort pointed me toward truth:
That my peace matters.
That my boundaries are valid.
That my self-respect is non-negotiable.
It reminded me: Love is not the same as self-abandonment.
Sometimes love looks like distance.

Sometimes healing begins with saying, *enough.*

Let discomfort be your guide, not your tormentor.
Let it point you toward the places that ache for attention, not
punishment. And above all, remember:
You are not broken for feeling this way.
You are becoming.
You are remembering.
You are returning to who you were always meant to be.

Relationships as Invitations

Every relationship is an invitation—not always to remain, not
always to agree—but always to see yourself more honestly.
Some people will illuminate your gifts. Others will stir your
wounds. Each serves a purpose.

Some will remind you of what's sacred to you. Others will press
against your edges, revealing where your boundaries need
reinforcing. Neither is accidental. Both are messengers.

Relationships are not simply roles we play—parent, friend,
partner, colleague—they are mirrors. Invitations.
Not to lose yourself, but to remember yourself.

Some connections arrive gently, wrapped in joy and ease.
Others arrive like storms—unsettling, intense, hard to hold.
And yet, each calls forth something within us that's ready to

surface. Patience. Truth. Courage. Letting go.

No experience is wasted when we learn to ask the deeper question:
"What is this showing me about myself?"
Not: *"Why did they do this to me?"*
But: *"What is this experience inviting me to notice, to feel, or to reclaim within myself?"*

Even the most painful dynamics can hold sacred invitations.
To speak up.
To step away.
To release the need to be understood.
To stop overextending yourself in the name of keeping the peace.
To stop shrinking in relationships that don't see the fullness of who you are.

Some people teach through their presence. Others through their absence. Both can leave a lasting imprint. This doesn't mean tolerating harm. It means recognizing when the most loving choice is to choose yourself.

Walking away isn't failure—it can be the moment you finally say yes to your own wholeness.

When we begin to view our relationships not as battles to win or losses to grieve, but as soul assignments—each offering a unique reflection—something softens. We stop clinging. We start listening. We let go with less bitterness and stay with more intention.

The relationship may not last. It may not heal.
But the version of yourself that emerges from it—
that's the real gift.

In the end, relationships are less about the other person and more about the evolution they invite in you.

Who are you being asked to become?
What truth are you being asked to reclaim?
What version of yourself is waiting to be loved—
by *you*—through this experience?

That is the invitation.

Holding the Mirror Lightly

This part isn't about blame. It's not about spiraling into over-analysis or dissecting every conversation as if it holds a secret code. It's about softening. About noticing, with gentleness, what stirs inside you when life brushes up against something tender.

Most of all, it's about compassion.

- Compassion for the parts of you still learning how to be seen.

- Compassion for the people who unknowingly act as your mirrors.
- Compassion for the process of becoming—imperfect, unfolding, real.

When we begin to see others as mirrors, we start recognizing how they reflect our hopes, our hurts, our gifts, and our growth edges. But sometimes we grip the mirror too tightly—trying to decode every nuance, find meaning in every discomfort, make sense of every emotional ripple.

The truth is: the mirror was never meant to be held like a microscope. It was meant to be held with care.
Lightly. Lovingly.

Seeing others as mirrors doesn't mean blaming yourself for their behavior. It doesn't mean mining every wound for spiritual meaning. Some pain has no profound lesson.
Some people act from their own unhealed places.

The mirror, in those moments, isn't a verdict—it's a whisper.
A possibility. An offering, not an obligation.

To hold the mirror lightly is to allow room for grace.
It's asking, *What might this be showing me about myself?*—and being okay if no answer comes right away. It's staying open without becoming overwhelmed. Curious without becoming consumed. It's also remembering: not every reflection is true.

Some mirrors are warped by someone else's story.
Some projections were never yours to carry.
And holding the mirror lightly helps you discern the
difference—with love, not guilt.

This is how we stay grounded.
This is how we free ourselves from the weight of
over-responsibility and the ache of internalized shame.

Spiritual awareness was never meant to be a burden—
it's a path of choice. Of clarity. Of compassion.

So let the mirror offer its insight, softly.
Let it reflect without wounding.
Let it guide you without gripping you.
And when it reveals something hard to witness, let your gaze
be tender. Hold yourself with the same lightness.
The same grace.

You're still learning.
Still becoming.
Still remembering who you were
before the world told you who to be.

That, too, is sacred.

Choose What Resonates

Not every reflection will land.

Not every insight will feel true for you—
and that's more than okay.

You are not here to agree with everything.
You're here to notice what stirs.
What softens. What resists. What speaks.

That, too, is part of your reflection.

This isn't a roadmap or a rulebook. It's an offering.
A perspective you can hold for a moment—or set down
entirely. It asks nothing of you but your presence.
It simply wonders:
"What might life be revealing to you, about you?"

As you stand before the mirrors others offer, remember:
You don't have to take every image to heart. You are not
required to translate every experience into meaning.
You do not need to claim what doesn't feel like yours.

The mirror isn't a command—it's a conversation.
It opens a door, not a demand.
It invites you to listen—not to obey.

And in that space, *resonance* becomes your compass.

Resonance is quiet. Subtle. True.
It shows up as a hum in your chest, a stillness in your breath, a
yes that has no words.

It doesn't need to justify itself—it simply *is*.
You'll know it when it finds you.
Just as surely, you'll know when something doesn't belong.

And that, too, is sacred.

Sometimes, we inherit reflections that were never ours. We
absorb projections from others—especially from those we long
to be seen by—and carry them like burdens.

But growth is not about pleasing; it's about *discerning*.
It's the quiet strength of saying, "That may be true for you,
but it's not mine."

You are allowed to walk away from mirrors that distort.
You are allowed to protect your truth.
You are allowed to listen to yourself first.

To choose what resonates is to return to your own center.
It's a quiet reclaiming of trust in your own knowing.
It's refusing to trade your intuition for acceptance,
your clarity for comfort.

It's remembering: you are the one who lives with your truth—
no one else can define it for you.

Resonance doesn't always roar. Sometimes it's a whisper.
Sometimes it arrives like lightning.

However it appears, it always points you back to yourself.
To the truth you already carry.
To the light you already are.

The mirror is always there.
But *your gaze*—how you choose to look, what you choose to
see—that is your power.

So let this be a reflection, not a requirement.
A gentle invitation, not a task.

When you feel a flicker of recognition in someone else—pause.
That spark may just be showing you a part of yourself you're
ready to meet. Because in the end, you are your own mirror,
too. And your reflection—when held with love—will always
guide you home.

Chapter 4

The Power of Unlearning

To know yourself, you must unlearn everything that was ever said about you by those who could not see you. —Nayyirah Waheed

In many spiritual traditions, the path to self-discovery isn't paved with more information—it's carved by releasing what isn't real. It's not about accumulating, but *undoing*. Unlearning. Peeling back the false identities, labels, and expectations that were never truly yours.

This is the quiet work of awakening: loosening the grip of beliefs that once shaped your sense of self but no longer feel true. Beliefs born from survival, upbringing, culture, or conditioning—now asking to be laid down.

Unlearning is how we return.
To our essence. To what's real.
To what's always been.

We are born into stories.
Stories about who we're supposed to be, what we should

believe, how we ought to act, speak, feel, and belong.

These stories often arrive before we've had a chance to say yes—or to say *no*. They are passed down through generations, wrapped in tradition, religion, education, and love. But love does not always equal truth.

Even the most well-meaning stories can become cages when they are followed without question. So the journey back to yourself begins with a single, powerful inquiry:
"What part of me is truly mine—and what was assigned to me?"

These are not casual questions. They are sacred keys.
They ask you to be still. To be honest. To get uncomfortable.
To see with clear eyes and feel with an open heart. To be willing to let go—not to lose yourself, but to *find yourself beneath the noise.*

This is not destruction.
This is remembering.
This is healing as becoming.

Just as the snake must shed its skin to grow, you, too, must release what no longer fits.

The roles you've played. The expectations you've carried. The voices in your head that sound like safety but feel like self-abandonment.

Letting Go to Grow

Who taught you who to be?

Whose approval shaped your choices?

Which parts of yourself have you hidden, silenced, or performed away just to feel safe, accepted, or worthy?

This chapter is an invitation to lay those layers down.

Not in shame, but in love. Not in rejection of your past, but in reclamation of your truth. Because so much of this journey isn't about becoming someone new. It's about unlearning everything that is *not you*.

Everything you were taught in fear,

absorbed in silence, or accepted in order to survive.

Everything that once protected you,

but now limits your becoming.

We grow up collecting beliefs like souvenirs — most of which were never truly ours. But now, with tender awareness, you can begin to ask:

"Do I still choose to carry this?"

"Does this belief reflect my truth — or just my past?"

Unlearning is not forgetting.

It's a sacred act of returning.

A conscious clearing to make space for the truth that is already within you.

Let it be gentle. Let it be sacred. Let it be yours.

What Are You Ready to Release?

Many of us move through life carrying inherited beliefs — quiet scripts passed down through family, culture, systems, and silence.

Beliefs about:

- Who we must be in order to be loved
- What is considered "normal," "successful," or "worthy"
- What spirituality should look like
- How the world works—and where we're allowed to belong within it
- What emotions are acceptable to feel, express, or even admit

These beliefs often go unexamined, not because they are true, but because they are familiar. But *familiar does not mean aligned.*

Unlearning invites us to pause—not in judgment, but in curiosity—and ask:
"Is this mine to keep?" or *"Is it time to let it go?"*

This is not about blaming those who came before you. This is about reclaiming your right to choose who you are becoming.

The spiritual path is not a fixed blueprint to follow, but a living, breathing unfolding—revealing itself with each step you take. And only you can walk it.

As you walk, you may find yourself questioning what you once held sacred:
Your definitions of love.
Your understanding of power.
Your image of the divine.
Your place in the world.

You may begin to ask:

"Do I believe this because it resonates—or because I've been afraid to question it?"

"Who might I be if I stopped trying to fit into other people's expectations?"

"What if truth isn't a concept to memorize, but a feeling to trust?"

These are not signs that you're lost.
They are signs that your soul is waking up.
You are no longer satisfied with borrowed truths.
You are beginning to remember.

You can only receive truth in the capacity that your mind and heart are open to it. That openness—that willingness to question and feel deeply—is the sacred beginning.

Unlearning is not erasure. It is emergence.

As you gently dismantle the beliefs and identities that no longer serve you, you make space for the truth that *has always lived within you*—waiting to be felt, known, and honored.

If you're willing to walk a path that hasn't been paved for you, you open yourself to seeing life from a perspective that is uniquely your own. That's the gift: *your own way of knowing.* Your own voice. Your own resonance.

Don't take my word for it.
This is your journey.
Observe. Question. Feel. Discern.

Truth doesn't ask for your obedience—it asks for your presence. And when you show up with openness, even the illusions of fear, ego, and attachment begin to fall away, revealing a deeper knowing beneath it all.

The truth is: who you are becoming has always been within you.

You are not behind.
You are awakening.

So let your intuition speak louder than your fear. Let what stirs your soul, softens your body, or brings tears to your eyes be your compass. That's your truth rising to the surface. That's your Self remembering itself.

So I ask again—with gentleness and love:
"What are you ready to release, so you can return to yourself more fully?"

And when the answer comes—whenever it comes—offer it gratitude. Even what felt heavy once protected you. Even the roles you've outgrown helped carry you here.
Now it's time.
Set it down.
And breathe.

You are safe to become.

The Ego's Resistance to Letting Go

Letting go *sounds* simple. But to the ego, it can feel like unraveling—like standing at the edge of a cliff without knowing what lies below. That's because, for the ego, surrender feels like death. And in a way, it is.

To step into the fullness of who you are becoming, something familiar must fall away. An old identity. A worn-out story. A way of being that once kept you safe—but no longer feels true. Letting go is not destruction—it is liberation. A soft death that clears the way for new life.

In this space, ego is not your enemy.
It is the part of you that learned to survive by controlling, performing, perfecting.

It was shaped in response to a world that often rewarded suppression and punished authenticity. It believes safety comes from staying small, predictable, approved of. So when you begin to question, to unlearn, to rise—ego panics.

It says:
- *But this is who I've always been.*
- *What will they think if I change?*
- *If I release this… what's left of me?*
- *What if I'm wrong, and this path isn't safe?*

The ego clings to the known—even when the known is painful. It prefers certainty, even when that certainty suffocates the soul. That's why the work of releasing isn't easy.
It can feel like you're breaking apart.
But you're not breaking.
You're breaking open.

You are not falling apart—you are falling *inward*.
You are letting go of illusion so that truth can rise.
You are peeling away layers that were never really you,
to reveal the radiant essence that always was.

Expect discomfort.
Expect resistance.
Expect the urge to retreat to the familiar.

But remember this:

Every time you surrender a false belief,
you create more space for your soul to breathe.
Every time you say yes to your truth,
the noise of fear begins to fade.

You are not your ego.
You are the presence that watches it. The still, compassionate
awareness that notices the fear without becoming it. The soul
is not afraid of change—*it knows change is the doorway home.*

So when ego resists, meet it gently.
Not with war, but with witness.
Ask it what it's trying to protect.
Thank it for its effort.
And let it know: *You're safe now.*

You no longer need the old masks.
You no longer need to prove or explain or shrink.
You no longer need to carry the story of who you thought you
had to be.

Letting go is not losing yourself—it's losing the layers that kept
you from seeing who you truly are.

Some days, the ego will grip tighter. That's okay.
Growth is not linear. Neither is awakening.
What matters is that you keep choosing resonance over rules,
alignment over approval, truth over familiarity.

Letting go is sacred.
Letting go is brave.
Letting go is how you return.

And if resistance rises—good. That means you're close to
something real. You're nearing the threshold of transformation.
The soul recognizes the moment, even if the mind trembles.

You are not becoming someone new.
You are remembering someone eternal.

So breathe.
Lean in.
Trust the unraveling.

Your soul already knows the way home.

The Lifelong Art of Unlearning

Unlearning isn't a single breakthrough.
It's a slow, sacred unfolding.
A rhythm, not a race.
A return, not a destination.

This journey doesn't happen all at once. You don't strip away
every false belief overnight and awaken fully formed, healed,
and whole. That's not how transformation works—
that's how perfectionism whispers.

But the soul speaks differently. It moves with patience. With grace. It evolves in seasons and spirals, inviting you again and again to come home to yourself.

You'll revisit old lessons through new lenses.
What once felt like truth may shift.
What once fit may no longer belong.
And that's not regression — that's revelation.

Truth is alive. And so are you.

Unlearning happens in quiet moments. In stillness. In the gentle sting of discomfort when something no longer aligns. In the pause before you respond. In the awareness that you've outgrown a reaction, a belief, a role.

You notice. You breathe. You choose differently — not because you've mastered the lesson, but because you're listening now.

Each time you soften a hardened belief,
Each time you choose your voice over approval,
Each time you trade performance for presence —
You are unlearning.

And with every unlearning, you are remembering.

There is no final version of you waiting at the end of this road.
There is only deeper and deeper truth.

A continual becoming.
A sacred invitation to peel back, open up, and return —
again and again.

This isn't something to dread.
It's something to celebrate.
Because lifelong unlearning means you are alive to your own
evolution—alive to growth, to grace, to possibility.

There is no shame in shifting.
There is power in your awareness.
There is freedom in saying:
"That used to serve me. It doesn't anymore. And that's okay."

Let your beliefs breathe.
Let your identity evolve.
Let yourself be surprised by what feels right now.

You're not broken.
You're not behind.
You're not failing.

You are growing—in rhythm, on purpose, and right on time.
So when the ego says, *"Are we still doing this?"*
You can smile and respond, *"Yes. And we're doing it more gently
this time."*

This is the sacred art of unlearning:

A cycle of releasing.
A practice of remembering.
A path of returning to what is real.

And as you grow, the world around you may shift.
Some relationships may loosen.
Some rooms may no longer hold you.
That doesn't mean you're alone—it means you're becoming.

The space between who you were and who you're becoming
can feel tender. But it is also sacred.
This in-between is where clarity emerges.
Where resonance begins to rise.

Some connections may fade—not from failure, but from
frequency. Some structures may fall away—not because you're
better than them, but because you're no longer willing to
abandon yourself to stay in them.
Let that be okay. Let yourself shed.

The more you unlearn, the more space you create for what
truly aligns. And in that space, slowly, gently—
your people will find you.
People who see you, not the mask.
People who honor your presence, not your performance.

You will co-create spaces where your truth can breathe.
Where your soul feels seen.

Where no part of you needs to shrink.

Yes, your path may narrow for a while—but it will open again.
Wider. Truer. Deeper.
Let that be your comfort:
This stretch of solitude is not an ending.
It is a clearing.
It is making room—for your peace,
your purpose, and your people.

Keep going.
Keep shedding what was never yours.
Keep choosing what resonates.

Your becoming is not just your own.
It is a call that brings others home, too.

Practical Steps for Unlearning

(...*that you get to define for yourself.*)
How incredible is that?

There is no universal roadmap for unlearning. That's both its
magic and its challenge. The path back to your own truth
doesn't come packaged with instructions. It calls for your
presence, your curiosity, and your willingness to listen
deeply—to the whispers of your own soul.

Teachers may show you a door, but it's yours to open. Yours to

walk through. Yours to explore as you chart your unique way forward, mastering your own limitations along the way.
I realized that many of the beliefs I held about how to live weren't truly mine. Yet I carried them as if they were, conditioned to wear them like armor—
until I chose to step out of that passive role.

I challenged what was handed to me, and took the pen to write my own story. Because what we believe becomes our reality— not simply because it's fact, but because we've accepted it, embraced it.

Growth happens when you reclaim your free will,
when you learn to think for yourself,
when you decide what truly resonates instead of simply inheriting what others told you to believe.

Unlearning isn't about swapping one set of beliefs for another. It's about creating space. It's about asking: *"Is this really mine?"*

Is this belief, this expectation, this identity or rhythm— something you chose consciously? Or is it something you absorbed, performed, or held on to out of habit or survival?

The "practical steps"—if we can call them that— aren't checklists or hard rules. They're gentle invitations.
Soft openings in your inner world, helping you see yourself more clearly beneath the layers of conditioning, perfectionism,

and people-pleasing.

They're reminders: you already carry the wisdom you need. You're not here to collect answers—you're here to remember your own.

So rather than offering formulas, I offer reflection. Rather than instructions, I offer space to feel. Here are a few gentle doorways—see which one stirs something within you:

- **Begin noticing.** Pay attention to moments when something feels off. When you feel tight, small, or disconnected. Unlearning often begins not with fireworks, but in these soft, quiet discomforts.

- **Ask your own questions.** Instead of "What should I believe?" try "What feels true to me right now?" Your truth is fluid. You are not bound to the version of yourself that said yes out of fear or conformity.

- **Give yourself permission to pause.** Sometimes the most radical act of unlearning is simply slowing down. Creating space to feel what's present instead of rushing to fix or change it.

- **Notice what drains and what nourishes you.** This can reveal which systems, roles, or identities you're ready to release—and which ones are calling you forward.

- **Let your body guide you.** The body often knows before the mind does. What do you sense in your gut, your heart, your breath? Truth has texture. Resonance has rhythm. Learn to listen deeply to your own.

Remember, unlearning doesn't always look dramatic.
Sometimes it's just quietly choosing a different response.
Sometimes it's simply not abandoning yourself this time.

There's no rush. There's no "getting it right."
This is your sacred unfolding. Your returning home.

Let what resonates stay.
Let what feels false gently fall away.
And let your own knowing be your compass.

You Are Not Broken. You Are Becoming.

This chapter isn't about fixing what's broken. It's about peeling back illusions. Unlearning is a remembering—of the truth that's always lived beneath the noise.

You are not your pain, your patterns, or your past.
You are the space beneath it all.
And that space?
It is sacred.

Chapter 5

Sacred Self-Discovery

The privilege of a lifetime is to become who you truly are.
—Carl Jung

Self-discovery is the key to real knowledge—urging you to look within rather than rely solely on external authorities. Real knowing doesn't arrive through noise, credentials, or someone else's approval. It unfolds in quiet moments of reflection, when you dare to listen inwardly. Sacred self-discovery is the gentle and ongoing process of peeling back layers that were never truly yours, and reconnecting with the essence that always was.

This journey isn't about fitting into anyone's definition of truth—it's about learning to recognize your own. While the world may offer frameworks or insights, only you can feel what resonates at the deepest level. And that resonance is powerful. It is what guides you back to yourself.

You Are the Journey and the Destination

Self-discovery isn't a destination you arrive at—it's a way of being. It's the unfolding of remembering, reclaiming, and reconnecting to who you are beneath the roles, the wounds, and the conditioning.

True self-discovery is sacred because it invites honesty, humility, and courage. It draws you into deeper alignment—not with what you've been told to be, but with who your soul already knows you are.

This journey isn't about perfection.
It's about presence.
It isn't about fixing yourself.
It's about finding yourself—layer by beautiful layer.

The path of self-discovery doesn't follow a straight line. It spirals. It loops. It pauses. It deepens. Sometimes it circles back before it moves forward. And through it all, you are not walking toward something outside yourself—you are returning to the home within, to the truth that's been there all along.

You are not separate from what you seek.
You are not incomplete until you find it.
You are the unfolding.
You are the wisdom.
You are the path.

The destination isn't some polished version of you—it's the soft, steady rhythm of self-trust. It's the rootedness in your own presence. It's a quiet resonance with the knowing that already lives inside you.

When you stop chasing external definitions of success or identity—and begin listening to what feels alive, grounded, and true within—you'll realize the answers were never "out there." They were always whispering from within, waiting for your trust.

So let this chapter remind you:
You are not behind.
You are not broken.
You are not unfinished.

You are the one walking, and the one being walked home to.
You are the sacred unfolding.
You are the journey and the destination.

Keep listening. Keep softening. Keep honoring what resonates.

It's not selfish to follow your truth.
It's self-honoring. It's liberation.
And it begins—always—with a return to yourself.

You are your own greatest mystery, and your own greatest guide.

Creating Sacred Space for Discovery

Sacred self-discovery doesn't demand a specific ritual,

religion, or roadmap. It begins with something simpler—and often harder to find in a noisy, demanding world: space.

Not just physical space, though that can help. It's the kind of space that invites you to simply *be* with yourself—without performing, pleasing, or proving. A space where you can gently exhale the weight of who you've been told to be, and softly ask, *Who am I, really?*

Creating sacred space is an act of devotion—not to something outside of you, but to the truth that lives within. It's not about perfection or discipline.

It's about presence. Permission. Grace.
It's giving yourself the freedom to slow down,
notice what you feel, and
explore without judgment or hurry.

This space doesn't require candles or silence—though it may include them. It might be found in a morning walk, the pages of your journal, the breath you take before you respond, or the brief moments you sit quietly with no agenda. It's any moment where you meet yourself with curiosity and compassion, with honesty and softness.

You don't need to know what will arise in this space.
You don't need answers. In fact, that's the point.

This space is for listening, not striving. For noticing what's present—not fixing it, but understanding it. It's making room for the subtle wisdom inside you to rise to the surface.

To deepen your journey, you might create rituals or practices that turn self-reflection into sacred time.

As your guide, I'm not here to tell you what you'll find in that space—nor would I want to. Only you can know what's true for you. What I offer is this:

- Make space for your truth to *speak*—not to perform.
- Let your questions breathe before rushing to answer them.
- Allow yourself to be in-process. That's where growth lives.

Sacred space is less about what surrounds you, and more about how you hold yourself within it. It's a reclaiming of your inner ground. A remembering that your inner world deserves care— that you don't need to earn your own presence.

Let these moments be yours. You don't need anyone else's permission to make your life feel sacred. This is your invitation—not to do more, but to be *with* yourself more deeply.

Whatever comes, trust that it's part of your becoming.
You are not here to follow someone else's map.
You are here to discover your own way—step by sacred step.

Honoring the Layers of Becoming

Sacred self-discovery isn't a race toward some final version of yourself. It's not about perfection, or ticking off milestones. Instead, it unfolds like a spiral—each turn inward revealing something ancient and essential that's been quietly waiting beneath the surface, long before you had words to name it.

At times, you'll revisit lessons you thought you'd mastered. This isn't failure—it's a sign that you're seeing the same truth from a deeper place: through wiser eyes, a more open heart.

Self-discovery is layered this way. It's cyclical, not linear. Messy, not mechanical. Human, not performative.

The deeper truth? You're not becoming someone new. You're peeling back the layers of conditioning, fear, and inherited beliefs to remember who you've always been beneath it all.

Meet each version of yourself with compassion. Each one was doing their best to survive, to belong, to love. You're not discarding them—you're welcoming them home.

Every step holds value.
Every version of you has wisdom to offer.

This is not a journey of escape. It's a journey of return.

Trusting the Wisdom Within

You don't need to earn your wisdom.
You don't need a title, a certification, or anyone's permission
to begin truly knowing yourself.

There is already a voice inside you that knows—
Not the voice shaped by fear, judgment, or performance,
But the quieter one.
The steady one.
The one that softly whispers, *"This feels right,"*
even when no one else understands why.

That voice is your inner wisdom. And it is sacred.

In a world that teaches us to outsource truth—to experts,
systems, traditions—it can feel radical to turn inward and
listen. But sacred self-discovery invites exactly that: a gentle
return to your own knowing.

This isn't about rejecting all outside guidance.
 It's about learning discernment.
Does this belief align with me?
Is this path one I choose—or one I inherited?
Trusting yourself again might feel uncertain at first.
That's okay.

Doubt doesn't mean you're lost—it means you're awake and
paying attention.

Let curiosity be your compass, not control.
Let resonance guide you, not rigid rules.
You are your own best guide.
You always have been.

Your inner wisdom may speak through sensation, image, dream, silence, or longing. It may arrive in fragments or in waves. However it comes, it is worthy of your trust.

You are not broken.
You are not behind.
You are more than qualified to know your own truth.

This chapter of self-discovery is about remembering what you were taught to forget:
The compass is already within you.

Welcoming the Unknown

Sacred self-discovery is never a straight line.
It's not a checklist of milestones or a series of perfect revelations. It is a mystery—unfolding in unexpected ways, on timelines we can't predict. And that is the beauty of it.

To welcome the unknown is to soften our grip on certainty. It's to say, *"I don't need to have it all figured out to keep going."*

In fact, the not-knowing is often where the most profound transformation begins. When you stop trying to control every

step, you open space for deeper truths to arise—
truths that come not from force, but from openness.

When you release the need for immediate answers, you start to trust the wisdom held in the questions themselves. You begin to trust life as a co-creator in your unfolding, not as something to be conquered or mapped.

Welcoming the unknown doesn't mean drifting aimlessly. It means walking with presence. Becoming fluent in the language of your inner landscape. Listening for resonance.
Noticing where your energy contracts and where it expands.
Distinguishing which uncertainties feel heavy—
and which feel like invitations.

Sometimes the unknown arrives as endings, confusion, or a sacred pause. It may feel like unraveling. But often, you're simply being emptied—so you can be filled anew.

The unknown is not a void. It is a doorway.

When you greet it with reverence instead of fear, it becomes a sacred ally. It reminds you that you are not here to remain the same. You are here to evolve. And you don't need to see the whole path to take the next step.

Let the mystery be your medicine. Let it stretch you open in ways that reveal more of who you truly are. Let it guide you not away from yourself—but deeper within.

The Mirror of Everyday Moments

Sacred self-discovery doesn't only happen on mountaintops, in silence, or through ceremony. More often, it reveals itself in the humblest places: in your morning breath, your daily commute, the irritation rising in a meeting, or the joy of an unexpected belly laugh.

The sacred is not separate from your life—it lives inside it.

Every moment is a mirror.
It reflects where you are, what you value, what triggers you, and what lights you up. It shows how you speak to yourself when no one is listening.

How your body tightens or softens in response to another's words. The small decisions you make each day, and the energy you bring to them. All of it is data.
All of it is a doorway.

Sacred self-discovery isn't about grand gestures—
it's about intimate honesty.
It asks:
"Can you be present with your reactions without judgment?"
"Can you meet your confusion with curiosity instead of shame?"
"Can you trust that even the mundane holds meaning?"

The sacred isn't something you arrive at once you've "gotten better" or "healed" enough. It is here, now—in this very moment you're living.

How you meet yourself in your daily life is the practice. Every missed opportunity, every pause instead of reaction, every clear yes or no—each is a brushstroke in the masterpiece of your becoming.

There is no need to escape ordinary life to find yourself. You are already in it. The question is: *"Are you willing to look closely?"*

Let your everyday experiences reflect you back—not as evidence of shortcomings, but as invitations to see where you're growing, where you're tender, and where your soul calls for deeper attention. Let them teach you to live from the inside out, moment by moment.

This is the essence of sacred self-discovery: the courage to change from within—not for appearances, but because you know your inner world shapes the outer one.

Mahatma Gandhi said,
"Be the change you wish to see in the world."
It's not a call to perfection—
but to presence.
To alignment.
To authenticity.
Seen this way, the sacred isn't somewhere you go.
It's how you choose to see.

Chapter 6

Finding What Resonates

To find yourself, think for yourself.
—Socrates

There is a quiet power in discovering what truly resonates within you—a gentle knowing that feels like coming home after a long journey. This chapter invites you to slow down and listen—not for answers handed down by others, but for the subtle stirrings of your own spirit. In a world overflowing with noise, expectations, and endless opinions, finding what resonates is an act of reclaiming your inner authority.

Self-discovery is not about fitting yourself into a mold or following someone else's map. It's about tuning in to the unique frequency of your own truth—the thoughts, feelings, and whispers that feel authentic, nourishing, and right. This resonance is your compass, your sacred signal guiding you toward alignment and clarity.

But resonance doesn't always arrive with fanfare or certainty. Sometimes it comes as a quiet pull, a moment of peace, or even a flicker of discomfort that invites you to look deeper.

Trusting what resonates means honoring your inner landscape without rushing to judge or dismiss. It means giving yourself permission to explore what feels meaningful—even when it challenges old beliefs or leads into unknown territory.

Within these pages, you're invited to become curious about what calls to you, what moves you, and what awakens your heart. This is a process of remembering—the wisdom you've always carried beneath the noise and expectations. It's an unfolding, a gentle unveiling of what is already true inside you.

As you continue reading, may you feel empowered to honor your own journey, trust your instincts, and embrace the unique path that emerges when you listen deeply. Finding what resonates is not a destination but a practice—a sacred dance between your inner knowing and the world around you.

This chapter is your invitation to step fully into that dance. To find your rhythm, your voice, your sacred yes. To discover what lights you up and what grounds you. To remember that your truth is enough. Always.

Your Truth Is Your Compass

In a world overflowing with teachers, methods, traditions, and opinions, how do you know what's right for you? You listen for what resonates—what speaks directly to your spirit.

Resonance isn't a matter of intellect or logic. It's energetic. It's that quiet, undeniable feeling of "yes." A cellular remembering. A sense of coming home.

Your path won't look like anyone else's—and it's not meant to. You are not here to follow a blueprint; you're here to write your own.

Explore freely, but don't get tangled in trying to "get it right." If a teaching feels heavy or off, gently set it aside. If it feels light and alive, follow it with trust.

Honor the wisdom flowing through your body, your emotions, your energy. Your inner compass knows the way.

What Resonance Feels Like

Resonance isn't something you can pin down with certainty or fit neatly into a definition. It is a feeling—an experience—a subtle signal moving through you in ways both tender and profound. It's less about logic or proof, and more about the quiet knowing that something fits, like a familiar song playing softly in the background of your soul.

You might notice resonance as a gentle stirring in your chest, a sense of ease settling over your mind, or a spark of curiosity inviting you to lean in closer. Sometimes it arrives as a soft breath of relief, lifting tensions you didn't even realize you were holding. Other times, it feels like a gentle tug or a deep pause—

a call to pay attention, to question, to feel more deeply.

Resonance often feels expansive, as if a small door inside you has opened, inviting in light and possibility. It can be both comforting and unsettling, nudging you toward something real and true—even if that truth feels unfamiliar or uncharted. This feeling isn't about immediate answers or instant clarity. It's an invitation to begin a conversation with yourself.

Notice that resonance doesn't always come with loud fanfare. Sometimes it whispers. Sometimes it shows up wrapped in contradiction, discomfort, or hesitation—a sacred pause.

These moments can be just as valuable as those filled with joy or peace. They invite you to sit with what arises, to hold space for questions without rushing toward solutions.

What matters most is that resonance honors your unique path. What deeply resonates for one person may pass unnoticed by another—and that is the beauty of it. There is no single right answer, no universal truth that fits all.

Your resonance is yours alone. It reflects your experiences, your soul's longings, and your evolving understanding.

This is why it matters to listen with openness and curiosity, rather than expectation. Resist the urge to label your experience as "right" or "wrong." Instead, see it as an unfolding dialogue between you and your inner world—a process that deepens with time, patience, and gentle attention.

As you move forward, I invite you to trust your sense of resonance as your guide—not because it's always clear or simple, but because it is authentic. Let it be a spark, a touchstone, a way to navigate the rich, often mysterious terrain of your self-discovery.

Above all, remember this: what resonates isn't something you find outside yourself. It is something you uncover within. It is the echo of your soul's truth, patiently waiting to be heard.

Listening to Your Inner Voice

Finding what resonates begins with a willingness to listen—not just to the chatter of the mind or the swirling opinions around you, but to the quiet, steady voice within. This inner voice isn't loud or demanding. It doesn't shout or command. Instead, it whispers in moments of stillness, nudges you through subtle feelings, and speaks in the language of intuition and knowing.

Learning to hear this voice takes practice and patience. It's like tuning a delicate instrument, requiring gentle attention and kindness toward yourself when distractions or doubts arise. Sometimes, the inner voice may feel faint or uncertain—especially if you've been taught to ignore it or question your own truth.

But this voice holds your deepest wisdom. It knows what feels true beneath the noise of expectations and fears. It's a compass that asks for no maps or directions, only trust.

As you cultivate the habit of listening, you begin to recognize the difference between what truly resonates inside and what is merely noise or obligation.

Remember, listening isn't about rushing toward answers or forcing clarity. It's about creating space for your own knowing to arise—patiently, without judgment. In this space, you give yourself permission to discover what lights you up and calls you forward—not because someone else says it should, but because your soul quietly agrees.

Recognizing Resistance and Discomfort

Finding what resonates isn't always easeful—and it's not always comfortable. Often, the very invitations that lead to deeper growth stir something unsettled within us. Discomfort, hesitation, even fear may rise when we approach the edges of what we've known, believed, or trusted.

But resistance isn't a red flag to turn back. More often, it's a quiet signal that something meaningful is stirring—something that may be asking you to release old stories, soften rigid patterns, or reimagine what's possible. Discomfort can act as a threshold, not a wall—a place where you're being gently asked to pause, pay attention, and choose with care.

Meeting resistance with curiosity instead of judgment can shift everything. Rather than pushing past it or silencing it, you might ask: *What is this feeling trying to reveal? What part of me is contracting—and why? Am I afraid to grow, to shed something familiar, or to be seen in a new way?*

At times, resistance may point to tender places—old wounds or deep conditioning. Other times, it's simply the natural unease that comes with expansion. Either way, it's part of the journey.

Discomfort isn't the opposite of resonance—it's often the doorway into it.

Leaning gently into these edges, without forcing yourself through, allows your self-awareness to grow. It helps you feel more clearly what is truly yours—and what is asking to be reimagined.

This path is not about pushing through or getting it "right." It's about welcoming all of you—especially the parts that hesitate— into the sacred unfolding of who you are becoming.

Distinguishing External Influence from Inner Knowing

One of the quiet but essential invitations on the path of resonance is learning to discern the difference between what comes from outside of you—and what arises from within. In a world overflowing with information, advice, and well-meaning perspectives, it can be easy to lose touch with your own inner voice.

External influence isn't inherently wrong. Often, it brings valuable insight, beauty, and inspiration. But when it begins to overshadow your intuition—when the volume of the world drowns out your own inner knowing—it can pull you away from what is most true for you.

The practice here is gentle discernment. It's the art of noticing: *Which thoughts or choices feel shaped by expectation or fear? And which feel rooted in something quieter—something steady, alive, and unmistakably your own?*

This isn't about rejecting wisdom or closing yourself off. It's about learning to recognize your own signal amidst the static. Like tuning a frequency, you begin to sense what resonates clearly—and what feels misaligned, even if it once made sense.

You might ask yourself:

"When I consider this belief or path, do I feel a sense of expansion or contraction?"

"Is this something I truly feel aligned with—or something I've absorbed to please, perform, or belong?"

"Does this choice bring me closer to myself, or further into a version of me shaped by someone else's vision?"

Inner knowing often doesn't shout. It arrives as a soft clarity, a subtle but unmistakable pull, or a quiet exhale that says: *yes, this is mine*. Trusting that voice takes time, especially when the world's noise feels urgent or persuasive.

With practice, that clarity grows. Remember—your truth is not static. It shifts, deepens, and evolves as you do. What feels aligned today may transform tomorrow.
That, too, is part of the unfolding.

By staying rooted in your own experience—rather than others' expectations—you reclaim the freedom to walk your path with presence, courage, and trust in what is real for you.

Allowing Space for Evolution

Finding what resonates is not a final destination—it's a living process. A quiet unfolding. A continual invitation to grow, shift, and expand in your own way, on your own time.

To honor this evolution, you must give yourself permission to change. To release what once felt certain. To revise your beliefs. To welcome new layers of understanding as they surface. This doesn't mean you've lost your way—it means you're deepening into it.

Growth is not a betrayal of your past truth. It's an affirmation that your truth is alive, capable of adapting and widening as you move through new experiences. Sometimes, what once fit beautifully may no longer feel quite right—and that's not failure. That's transformation.

This kind of evolution asks for tenderness. For patience. It asks you to be kind to yourself when you feel unsure, when old patterns reappear, or when the path ahead seems blurry.

Growth isn't always linear. It spirals. It stumbles. It pauses and begins again.

Allowing space for your evolution means trusting the tempo of your own becoming—not rushing to answers or outcomes, but listening for what wants to emerge next. It means meeting change with curiosity rather than control, with compassion rather than judgment.

Sacred self-discovery isn't about reaching a flawless state. It's about being fully present with who you are now, while staying open to who you're still becoming. The invitation is to hold your journey with softness, knowing that your inner compass will continue to adjust as you do.

When you give yourself space to evolve, you create room for new resonance to find you. You stay connected to what's real, what's changing, and what's quietly guiding you forward— step by step.

Practical Ways to Explore Resonance

Exploring what truly resonates with you is a deeply personal, unfolding journey. There's no single path to follow — no checklist that fits all. Instead, consider these as gentle invitations — sparks of possibility to help you stay curious and connected as you listen inward.

- **Pause and Notice**
  Throughout your day, take quiet moments to check in with yourself. What thoughts or experiences feel expansive? Which ones bring tension, resistance, or a quiet "no"? These subtle signals are meaningful — clues guiding you closer to your truth.

- **Ask Open-Ended Questions**
  Bring a spirit of gentle inquiry to your inner world. Ask questions like, "What feels true for me right now?" or "What draws my interest or energy?" Let the questions linger without rushing for answers. Often, resonance speaks in whispers that surface over time.

- **Experiment with Openness**
  Try new ideas or practices with a sense of curiosity and softness. Pay attention to how they land in your body, heart, and breath. Do they feel light, tight, neutral, or nourishing? Even a "no" carries wisdom — it helps you refine what feels aligned.

- **Journal Your Journey**
  Let writing be a sacred space for reflection. Use your journal to track insights, longings, questions, and hesitations. Over time, patterns may begin to emerge—threads of resonance weaving through your lived experience.

- **Create Rituals of Presence**
  Small, meaningful pauses—like a slow breath before your day begins or a quiet moment after a conversation—can help you stay grounded and attuned. Rituals don't need to be elaborate; they only need to feel sincere and supportive.

- **Hold Space for Silence**
  Sometimes the deepest clarity arises not through doing, but through simply being. Give yourself permission to sit in silence without trying to solve or decide anything. In that stillness, your inner voice may gently rise to meet you.

Remember, these are not rules or requirements—they're invitations. Let your exploration be fluid, playful, and kind. Trust that your resonance will unfold in its own rhythm, in ways uniquely true to you.

This journey is yours—and that is its sacred power.

Chapter 7

Evolving With Grace

You do not just wake up and become the butterfly
—growth is a process.
—Rupi Kaur

rowth is not always loud. Often, it arrives quietly—through softened edges, surrendered expectations, or a gentle pull to become more fully who you already are. In this chapter, we explore what it means to allow your e volution to unfold with grace—not as something forced or perfected, but as something deeply human, alive, and sacred.

To evolve with grace is to hold space for your becoming. It is the practice of loosening your grip on rigid stories and honoring the natural rhythms of change. It invites you to meet yourself with compassion in the in-between places—where old truths no longer fit, and new ones are still taking shape.

This chapter isn't about striving or self-improvement. It's about softening into the truth that growth can be gentle. It can be kind. And it can unfold without needing to be earned or proven. Here, you're invited to trust the wisdom of your own

unfolding—to honor both stillness and movement—
and to allow your path to emerge one step, one breath at a time.

You Are Allowed to Change

As you grow—spiritually, emotionally, mentally—you will
evolve. Your values may shift. Your boundaries may
strengthen. Your relationships may change. This is not a
problem; it's proof that you're alive and awakening.

Evolution doesn't ask you to be hard on yourself. It calls for
grace—the capacity to love yourself through transition, to
forgive yourself as you release outdated patterns, and to honor
who you have been along the way.

You are not meant to stay the same.
Even if others expect it.
Even if you once expected it of yourself.

Change is not a betrayal of who you were—it's an honoring of
who you're becoming.

Too often, we carry silent pressure to stay consistent: to cling to
old beliefs, maintain familiar roles, or keep showing up in ways
that no longer feel aligned. But your growth is not a problem to
fix—it is a truth to embrace.

You are allowed to outgrow what once felt like home.
You are allowed to evolve beyond what once made sense.

What resonated deeply in one season may no longer fit in the next. That doesn't mean you were wrong before. It means you were honest then—and you're being honest now.

Graceful evolution begins with permission: permission to change, not just outwardly but in the quiet shifts within—your values, your desires, your truths. This kind of change is often slow and subtle.

It may come as a whisper of discontent, a sudden clarity, or a growing sense that something no longer aligns. It may ask you to release what you once held tightly. It may ask you to listen more deeply to the version of yourself just beginning to emerge.

Yes—change may come with grief. Even when we know something is right, letting go can still feel tender. That too is part of evolving with grace: holding space for both the sorrow of release and the excitement of rebirth.

You can honor what was while making room for what wants to be.

Trust that your inner knowing is wise and alive.
Trust that your path is allowed to twist, pause, and redirect.
Trust that you do not need to justify your transformation to anyone—not even to yourself.

You are allowed to change.

You are allowed to choose again.
You are allowed to listen to the quiet call of your becoming,
even if no one else hears it yet.

This is not abandonment.
This is alignment.
This is you, returning more fully to yourself.

Growth Isn't Always Linear

We're often taught to measure growth by forward motion —
step by step, milestone by milestone. But true evolution rarely
follows a straight path. Sometimes, we circle back to familiar
lessons, old wounds, or past patterns — not because we've
failed, but because we're deepening. What once felt resolved
may reopen so we can meet it with greater wisdom, tenderness,
or simply from a new place within ourselves.

Growth often moves in spirals, not straight lines. You might
revisit the same emotional landscape time and again, but each
time, you bring a different version of yourself. This is not
regression — it's integration.

To evolve with grace is to release the pressure to "always move
forward." It's to trust that even the pauses, the plateaus, and the
seeming setbacks are part of your sacred unfolding. Progress
isn't always visible, and healing doesn't always follow a set
schedule. But that doesn't make it any less real.

Grace lives in the loops, not only the leaps.
You are growing, even when it doesn't look like it.
Even when you can't yet name it.

Trust that every step—every spiral—is drawing you closer to your truth.

Letting Go of Old Identities

As you grow, some parts of yourself naturally no longer fit—not because they were wrong, but because you've outgrown them. Old roles, labels, and identities that once felt safe or defining may start to feel confining.

You might catch yourself whispering, *"I'm not sure this is me anymore."* And that's perfectly okay. Letting go of an old identity is not a betrayal of who you once were—it's an honoring of who you are becoming.

The self you built may have been shaped by survival, expectation, or love. It may have helped you feel seen, accepted, or in control. But grace invites you to release what no longer serves you, even if it once brought comfort. It reminds you that you are allowed to shift, to soften, to expand beyond the boundaries of past definitions.

This shedding process can feel tender, even disorienting. You may wonder, *"If I'm not who I've always been, then who am I now?"* But evolution asks for trust before clarity. It's in the in-between—the space between who you were and who you're becoming—that deeper truths begin to emerge.

Letting go creates room for resonance.

And in that space, something new can take root—something more aligned, more authentic, more you.

Honoring the In-Between

There is a sacredness in the in-between—the space after something has ended but before something new has fully begun. It's the pause between breaths, the dusk before nightfall, the stillness that holds both release and possibility. Often, this space can feel uncomfortable. Uncertain. Like waiting in the dark for a light you cannot yet see.

But this liminal space is far from empty. It is rich with becoming.

To honor the in-between is to give yourself permission to not have all the answers. To resist the urge to rush toward clarity or force a conclusion. It is to trust that this tender space of not-knowing is part of your unfolding—not a detour from it.

In a culture that prizes urgency and arrival, it's easy to undervalue this phase. Yet true evolution rarely unfolds in neat, linear lines. It happens in the slow rewiring of thought, the quiet loosening of old beliefs, the invisible turning of the soil before anything blooms.

When you honor the in-between, you honor your own
becoming.

This is where your inner knowing deepens,
where trust takes root, and
where grace meets you with gentle hands,
whispering: You don't have to hurry. You're not lost.
You're just becoming.

Choosing Integrity Over Approval

There comes a moment in every journey of becoming when you
are invited to choose: the comfort of others' approval, or the
clarity of your own integrity.

Approval can feel safe. It soothes the parts of you that long to
belong, to be seen as "good" or "right." But the need to be
approved—especially when it costs you your truth—can slowly
pull you away from yourself. It can keep you performing a
version of who you think you should be, instead of honoring
who you truly are.

Choosing integrity over approval doesn't mean rejecting
community or ceasing to care about your impact. It means your
choices begin with inner alignment. It means asking:
*"Is this true for me? Does this reflect what I value, believe, and know
deep in my bones?"*

Sometimes, this choice will be quiet. Other times, it may feel like a rupture—especially if those around you have grown accustomed to a version of you that no longer fits. But integrity doesn't demand perfection or performance. It simply asks that you stay close to what's real.

Choosing integrity is choosing to live in resonance with your values, your knowing, and your soul's direction—even when it costs you validation.

This choice is courageous. And over time, it becomes freeing. Because every time you act from integrity, you reclaim a little more of yourself. You become rooted not in how others see you, but in how you see and honor yourself.

Grace meets you here too—not in being liked, but in being whole.

Welcoming New Truths Without Shame

As you evolve, you may uncover truths that challenge what you once believed—about the world, about others, and most intimately, about yourself. This unfolding is not a betrayal of who you were; it is a sign that you're alive, growing, and listening more deeply to what resonates now.

It's easy to look back and judge former versions of yourself— wishing you had known sooner, chosen differently, or seen more clearly. But shame can close the door on transformation. It tethers you to the past, punishing the part of you that was simply doing the best it could with the awareness it had. Welcoming new truths means making room for evolution without harshness. It is a radical act of compassion to say, *"I didn't know then, but I know now—and I choose to honor that."*

You are not meant to stay the same. Beliefs that once brought comfort may later feel constraining. Roles you once played may feel misaligned. Even dreams you once held dear may shift as you come into deeper relationship with your true self.

This doesn't mean you were wrong. It means you're waking up. And each awakening brings the chance to soften, release judgment, and make space for your becoming.

Let new truths arrive like honored guests—not with shame, but with curiosity. Let them sit with you, speak to you, and reshape you. Trust that your soul knows how to hold both who you've been and who you're becoming—with grace.

The Role of Self-Compassion

If evolution is the path, then self-compassion is the steady companion walking beside you—offering courage and tenderness with every step.

Change—especially the kind that happens inside—can bring uncertainty, vulnerability, and grief. You might find yourself revisiting old wounds, questioning familiar roles, or facing truths you weren't ready to see before.

These moments are not signs of weakness; they are sacred thresholds of transformation. Self-compassion invites you to meet those thresholds with softness instead of shame, with care instead of criticism.

Instead of asking, *"Why am I not further along?"* try asking, *"How can I be kind to myself here?"* Instead of pushing aside doubt or fear, welcome them to sit beside your growing wisdom. Speak to yourself with the same gentleness you would offer to someone you love.

This isn't about avoiding the hard things—it's about refusing to abandon yourself in the midst of them.

Your evolution won't always be graceful or clear. There will be stumbles, circles, and slow awakenings.

Self-compassion reminds you that none of it disqualifies you from being whole, worthy, or wise. Often, it is through the messiness that deeper truths take root.

Let yourself be held—not only by others,
but by your own kindness.
Let grace find you in the places that feel most tender.
Let compassion guide your steps as you grow into who you are becoming.

Celebrating Your Becoming

There is power in pausing to acknowledge just how far you've come. In a world that rushes from one milestone to the next, it's easy to overlook the quiet, inner shifts—the moments of clarity, the boundaries honored, the truths spoken, the small but sacred steps toward wholeness. But your becoming deserves to be witnessed—not only when it feels complete or polished, but exactly as it's unfolding.

Growth isn't only about reaching a final version of yourself— it's about recognizing and celebrating who you are becoming along the way. Celebrate the courage it took to question what no longer fits. Celebrate the softness you've nurtured, the self-trust you're reclaiming, the wisdom you now carry.

Even when the journey feels unfinished—or especially then— there is something deeply worth honoring. Celebration becomes a form of self-blessing, a quiet way of saying: I see you. I honor your becoming. I trust your path.

It doesn't need to be loud or public. It can be simple and intimate—lighting a candle, whispering a thank you, or placing your hand over your heart in recognition of your resilience.

Let celebration be an act of remembrance—of how beautifully human you are, and how worthy your unfolding continues to be. This is what it means to evolve with grace—not by rushing toward perfection, but by tenderly honoring each step, each season, each moment of becoming.

As you continue to evolve, know this: you are not just the student of your journey—you are also the teacher. Every challenge, every insight, every moment of stillness has been preparing you to listen more deeply to your own wisdom. You don't have to wait for someone else to name your truth. You are allowed to trust what you know. You are allowed to lead yourself home.

Chapter 8

Becoming Your Own Teacher

I have been a seeker and I still am, but I stopped asking the books and the stars. I started listening to the teaching of my Soul.
—*Rumi*

There comes a moment on the path of becoming when the noise around you quiets—and the voice within begins to rise. This chapter is about learning to trust that voice. Not because it holds every answer, but because it carries the questions only you are meant to live into.

Becoming your own teacher isn't about knowing everything. It's about recognizing your lived experience as a source of wisdom. It's about listening inward with curiosity, gentleness, and grace.

In a world that urges us to look outward for permission or proof, this is a radical return—to your inner knowing, your evolving truth, your sacred rhythm of becoming.

You are not behind. You are becoming. And every step you take toward deeper self-trust brings you closer to your wholeness

The Answers You Seek Are Within

There's a quiet wisdom that lives within you—beneath the noise of expectations, beneath the inherited scripts and the surface roles you've been asked to play. It may speak in nudges, sensations, or the subtle tug of curiosity. It may sound less like instruction and more like a gentle remembering. But it's there. It always has been.

The journey of becoming your own teacher begins with a radical act of trust: listening inward.

We are often taught to look outside ourselves for truth—to defer to experts, traditions, or systems that promise certainty. And while guidance can be meaningful, it can never replace the knowing that is uniquely yours.

You are not a blank slate waiting to be written on. You are a living, breathing archive of experience, intuition, and soul memory. Your life is its own curriculum.

To trust that the answers you seek are within is not to dismiss the world—it's to reclaim your role as an active participant in your unfolding. It's the shift from asking, *"What should I do?"* to *"What resonates with my deepest truth?"*

It's recognizing that resonance is a form of wisdom—and that your body, your spirit, your heart know how to feel it.

Sometimes, answers arrive slowly. They come in layers—through persistent questions, quiet reflections, or the sacred discomfort that signals something is ready to shift.

You don't need immediate clarity to honor what's moving within you. You only need the willingness to stay open, present, and compassionate with yourself along the way.

When you begin to see yourself as a source of truth, everything changes. You stop outsourcing your worth. You stop contorting yourself for approval.

You begin to walk with a steadiness—not because you know all the answers, but because you trust yourself to recognize them when they come.

This is not the end of learning. It's the beginning of a deeper kind—learning that honors your rhythm, your wisdom, your becoming. And as this trust grows, you may find that what you were seeking all along was not outside of you—but within, patiently waiting to be heard.

Let this be your invitation:
To return to yourself with reverence.
To trust what resonates.
To remember that the most powerful guide you will ever have is already within you.

This is where empowerment begins.
This is where sovereignty lives.
This is where you stop searching for "the way" —
and begin walking *your* way.

You are your own healer.
Your own guide.
Your own sacred authority.

This doesn't mean you won't ever need support. But it does
mean you no longer abandon your truth to receive it.

The Curriculum of Experience

There is a quiet knowing woven into every moment you've
lived. The lessons of your life aren't always loud or obvious—
often, they arrive disguised as missteps, detours, heartbreaks,
or even the stillness of ordinary days. But if you pause and
look closely, you'll begin to see: each season has carried
wisdom. Each experience has shaped your capacity to feel, to
choose, to grow.

Becoming your own teacher doesn't require perfection or
enlightenment. It simply asks that you honor what your life has
already taught you. That you begin to trust the insights born
not from books or external advice, but from the depth of your
own becoming.

You've survived what once felt unbearable.

You've softened where you once held walls.
You've leaned into healing, even when the path was unclear.

These are not small things. They are evidence of a deeper
intelligence moving through you—quiet, steady, and real.

When you stop dismissing your past and start listening to it
with reverence, you begin to remember:

You are already wise.
You are already carrying truths that no one else can speak in
quite the way you can.

You don't need to start over.
You need to start trusting.

"Your story is not your shame. It's your source material."

You are the student, yes. But you are also the source.

This is the power of lived experience.
This is the quiet authority of becoming your own teacher.

The Voice Within

There is a voice within you that has always known.
Not the loud, fear-driven voice shaped by self-doubt or
inherited expectations—but the quieter, steadier one beneath
it. The voice of inner knowing. The one that speaks truth
before your mind has a chance to second-guess it.

Becoming your own teacher means returning to that voice. Learning how it sounds. Learning to trust it—even when it defies logic, tradition, or the opinions of others. Especially then.

This voice doesn't shout. It invites.

This voice speaks in sensation, in dreams, in quiet nudges or persistent tugs on your heart. Sometimes, it emerges in stillness. Other times, it rises in resistance. Like any sacred relationship, it deepens with time, presence, and care.

It begins with listening—not for certainty, but for resonance. It's the daily practice of asking:
"What feels true for me right now?"
"What part of me is speaking—and what part is being silenced?"

So much of this journey is about unlearning the noise of external authority, and re-learning the sound of your own soul.

Let your inner voice become your compass—not to control, but to guide you with tenderness. And if that voice feels distant, trust that it hasn't left you. It's simply waiting—for quiet, for presence, for your return.

"Your inner voice isn't lost—it's just been buried beneath what you were taught to believe."

The more you choose to listen inward, the more you remember:

You are not without guidance.
You are not without wisdom.
You already carry the teacher you've been seeking—
quietly, faithfully, within you.

There Is No Final Arrival

Becoming your own teacher doesn't mean you'll always have the answers. It means you're willing to stay in relationship with the questions.

We live in a culture that glorifies certainty and arrival—as if wisdom is a destination you reach and never have to leave. But real growth is cyclical. Real learning is layered. There will be seasons when you feel deeply rooted in your knowing—and others when everything you thought you understood begins to shift again.

This isn't failure.
This is expansion.

Embracing the ongoing nature of learning allows you to meet life with more grace, and less pressure. It frees you from the illusion of being "done," and invites you into a deeper rhythm—one that honors change, nuance, and the sacred work of unlearning.

You may return to the same truth more than once—
each time receiving it more fully.

You may outgrow beliefs that once felt essential.
You may discover that even uncertainty holds its own quiet wisdom.

When you honor learning as a lifelong unfolding, you make space for your evolution without shame. You begin to trust the ebb and flow of your inner growth, rather than resist it.

"You are not meant to be static. You are meant to keep becoming."

This path is not about mastering life.
It's about meeting it—
with humility, with curiosity, with heart.

Being your own teacher means becoming a lifelong student of your own becoming.

It means trusting that the journey *is* the wisdom.

Chapter 9

Living Aligned and Awake

The privilege of a lifetime is to become who you truly are.
—Carl Jung

There comes a point in the journey when awakening shifts from a fleeting moment into a steady way of being. To live aligned and awake isn't about perfection or having constant clarity—it's about presence. It's about choosing, again and again, to honor what feels true, even when it's inconvenient, confusing, or misunderstood.

Living aligned is a practice of integrity with your soul. It invites you to listen more deeply, to move more honestly, and to stop sacrificing yourself for the sake of belonging. Awakening, in this way, is less about discovering something new and more about returning to what has always been within you: your inner knowing, your quiet courage, your ability to live a life that feels truly your own.

This chapter is an invitation to notice where you've been running on autopilot—and to come home. Not to someone else's idea of purpose or power, but to your own rooted truth.

This is where alignment begins. This is where awakening becomes fully embodied.

Spiritual Growth in Everyday Life

Spiritual growth doesn't always show up in grand rituals, retreats, or sudden revelations. More often, it lives quietly in the spaces between—in how you speak to yourself in the mirror, how you respond when plans unravel, how you choose to show up when no one else is watching.

It's easy to imagine awakening as a distant goal or dramatic event, something earned only through intense study or extraordinary experiences. But true spiritual growth is intimate, often subtle, and always unfolding. It moves with the rhythm of your daily life—in the way you listen, how you love, how you come back to yourself after wandering away.

To live aligned and awake means allowing your inner truth to shape your outer choices. It means honoring what resonates with your spirit, even when it challenges convention. You find it in the courage to set boundaries that protect your peace, in the gentle grace with which you forgive yourself, and in the willingness to recognize the sacred woven into the ordinary.

Spirituality isn't about floating away from your life.
It's about embodying your truth in a grounded, real way.
You don't have to live perfectly.
You only need to live awake.

You don't need to escape your life to grow spiritually—
you only need to show up more fully to it.

Spiritual growth isn't about performing goodness or chasing
perfection. It's about remembering your wholeness.
It's about recognizing your intuition as a valid guide,
your lived experience as sacred text, and your body as a wise
keeper of truth even before your mind catches on.

Everyday life becomes your classroom. Presence becomes your
practice. And your own unfolding becomes the path.

Let this be your reminder:
You don't need to chase enlightenment.
You are already walking with it—
in how you listen,
in how you choose,
in how you trust what calls you home.

What Alignment Feels Like

Alignment is not just an idea—it's a felt experience. A quiet
resonance deep in your body. A subtle clarity humming
beneath the surface of things. You don't recognize it because
someone else tells you you're on the right path, but because
something inside you exhales when you are.

It might feel like ease, even when the choice is hard.
It might feel like peace, even when the outcome is uncertain.

It might feel like a soft yes rising in your chest,
or the absence of that heavy, dragging no.

So much of life teaches us to ignore this inner compass. We're trained to silence the subtle knowing that lives in our bones in favor of logic, approval, or fear. But your body remembers. Your soul knows.

Sometimes alignment feels like expansion—your heart opening, your breath deepening, your energy flowing freely. Other times, it feels like simplicity, stillness, or silence. Like coming home to yourself.

Misalignment feels very different. It often shows up as:
- tension gripping your body,
- a racing or anxious mind,
- quiet resentment or exhaustion,
- or the soft ache of self-abandonment.

These aren't failures—they're signals. Invitations. Messages from within, asking you to pause, to reassess, to come back.

Living aligned and awake means tuning in to those signals. It means making space to ask:
"Does this feel like truth—or obligation?"
"Am I shrinking to fit someone else's version of me?"
"Where does my "yes" come from—love or fear?"

With time, you learn that alignment isn't a luxury—it's a guide.

A sacred rhythm flowing through your life, gently redirecting you back to yourself, again and again.

You don't have to get it perfect.
You only have to notice.

Awake Doesn't Mean Always Enlightened

Being awake is not about perpetual bliss. It's not about having all the answers or living in constant peace. Often, being awake means you feel more—not less. More nuance. More discomfort. More awareness of what no longer fits.

Awakening isn't a destination—it's a way of being with life. It's choosing to show up with presence and honesty, even when things are messy, uncertain, or painful. It's about being real, not perfect.

There will be days when you fall into old patterns, say yes when you mean no, or numb what you're not ready to face. That doesn't make you any less awake. In fact, the noticing itself is the awakening. The return is the practice.

To be awake is to:
- pause before reacting,
- question stories you've outgrown,
- honor the quiet truths that surface when you stop performing.

It's being willing to hold both clarity and confusion, courage and vulnerability, truth and tenderness.
It's realizing that wholeness includes all of you—
not just the polished, "spiritual" parts.

Awakening doesn't separate you from others; it softens you toward them. It invites compassion—
for yourself and for the world.
It allows you to say:
I don't have it all figured out—
but I am here.
I'm listening.
I'm learning.
I'm willing to begin again.

There's no checklist for being awake. There is only the slow, sacred process of returning to what is real for you—
moment by moment.

Inner Authority vs. External Validation

Living aligned and awake invites you to come home to your own inner authority—the quiet, unwavering sense of self that knows your truth beneath the noise of the world. This is where your values, feelings, and wisdom reside, patiently waiting for your attention and trust.

In contrast, external validation is the habit of seeking approval, acceptance, or worth from outside sources—whether that's people, systems, or cultural expectations. It's a natural human pattern, especially in a world that often measures success by how well you fit in or meet others' standards. But leaning too heavily on external validation can lead you away from your true path.

External validation asks you to perform, to please, to conform — often at the cost of your own peace and authenticity. When you live for someone else's applause, you risk losing the subtle, sacred signals of your own inner compass.

Discovering and trusting your inner authority is a revolutionary act of reclaiming your sovereignty. It means:

- Listening deeply to what feels right for you, even when it contradicts popular opinion or outside pressure.
- Honoring your boundaries and needs without apology.
- Valuing your intuition and emotional wisdom as vital guides.

This doesn't mean rejecting feedback or community. Instead, it means weighing external input through the filter of your own truth—choosing what nourishes your growth and releasing what no longer serves you.

Learning to distinguish inner authority from the pull of external validation is a practice—a daily invitation to pause and ask:
"What feels true to me right now?"
"Am I acting from fear of judgment, or from a place of alignment?"

As you cultivate this relationship with your inner authority, you become less dependent on others' opinions and more anchored in your own light. You begin to walk through the world with quiet confidence—not because you have it all figured out, but because you trust yourself to navigate whatever comes your way.

This shift isn't always easy. Old habits of people-pleasing or self-doubt can be persistent. But each time you choose your own voice over the crowd's, you grow stronger, freer, more awake.

Your inner authority is your sacred guide. It is the source of your deepest wisdom and the foundation of living a life that feels truly yours.

The Power of Intention in Daily Living

Living aligned and awake begins with intention—a conscious choice to bring presence and purpose to each moment. Intention is the bridge between your inner world and the life you create. It's not about rigid goals or perfection; it's about setting a tone of awareness and direction that honors your values and deepest desires.

When you live with intention, you become an active participant in your own unfolding, rather than a passive passenger swept along by circumstance. Each day offers countless opportunities to choose how you engage with the world—to respond rather than react, to prioritize what matters most, and to cultivate habits that nurture your growth.

Intentions don't have to be grand or complicated.
They might be as simple as:

- Approaching the day with kindness toward yourself.
- Choosing to listen fully in conversations.
- Taking a moment to breathe and center before a challenging task.

These small acts accumulate, shaping your experience and shifting your energy in profound ways.

The practice of setting intention invites you to pause and ask:

"What do I want to bring into this moment?"

"How can I align my actions with my authentic self?"

This reflective pause rewires your mind and heart to focus on what truly matters, instead of drifting into autopilot or reacting to external demands.

Living with intention also means embracing flexibility. Sometimes your path shifts, and your intentions evolve with it—and that's part of the growth. The key is to stay connected to your "why," the deeper purpose that fuels your journey. When intention guides your daily living, life feels less like a series of tasks and more like a meaningful dance with possibility. You begin to notice the subtle ways your inner world shapes your outer reality—and you reclaim the power to choose how you show up.

In this way, intention is not just a tool; it's a spiritual practice—a way of waking up to the sacredness woven into everyday life.

Integration: Living What You Know

Living aligned and awake is not only about discovery—it's about integration. It's the delicate art of bringing your inner truths into your everyday life, allowing your insights to shape your actions, choices, and relationships. Integration is where knowing meets being, where wisdom becomes lived experience.

Too often, we gather knowledge or have moments of clarity that remain fragmented—ideas held in our minds but not embodied in our lives. Integration asks us to bridge that gap: to live what we know, even when it feels challenging, uncomfortable, or at odds with others' expectations.

This process requires patience and gentle persistence. It's not about instant transformation or perfection; it's about continual alignment—choosing again and again to embody your values, your lessons, and your deeper self.
Integration means embracing your whole self, including shadows and contradictions. It's the willingness to face what's difficult while holding compassion for where you are in the

process. It's honoring the messy, imperfect journey just as much as the moments of clarity and grace.

When you live what you know, you step fully into your own power and authenticity. Your life becomes a reflection of your inner wisdom, creating harmony between your thoughts, feelings, and actions. This alignment radiates outward, influencing your environment and those around you in subtle, profound ways.

Remember, integration is not a destination—it's a lifelong dance. Each day offers new opportunities to practice, course-correct, and deepen your commitment to living aligned and awake.

Let this be your ongoing invitation:
trust yourself enough to live fully in the truth you carry,
honor your evolving path, and
celebrate the courage it takes to be both student
and teacher of your own life.

Chapter 10

You Are Already
Who You've Been Seeking

What you seek is seeking you.
—Rumi

This chapter invites you to pause and recognize a truth often overlooked beneath our searching: the person you've been seeking has always been within you. Spiritual growth is not about finding something new outside yourself—it's about remembering what has quietly lived inside all along—a steady, radiant presence waiting patiently beneath the surface.

You don't need to chase or become anything more; you are already whole, already enough. This is not a destination to reach but a gentle unfolding—
a reclaiming of your inner authority and wisdom.

In this chapter, we explore what it means to come home to yourself, to honor the depths you carry, and to live fully aligned with the quiet truth that has been guiding you all along.

Coming Home to Yourself

The most profound journey you will ever take is the one that leads you back to yourself. It's not about becoming someone new or reaching a distant goal—it's about remembering who you already are beneath the noise, doubts, and stories.

To come home to yourself is to settle into the quiet knowing that you are whole and complete, just as you are.

This is an invitation to rest in your own presence—a place where your heart breathes easier, your mind softens, and your spirit finds peace. Here, you recognize the sacredness of your existence and realize that the love, guidance, and answers you seek have always been within you.

Coming home means turning inward with kindness and patience, listening deeply to the voice that knows your values, fears, dreams, and passions. It's embracing your wholeness, even when parts feel rough or unfinished, and knowing you are enough—not because you've earned it, but simply because you exist.

This journey is not always easy or straight.
Sometimes it means facing shadows and discomfort, but with each step, you grow stronger and more clear, learning to trust your own rhythm instead of the scripts others hand you.

Coming home to yourself is an act of radical self-love and

courage—a letting go of chasing external validation to find peace in the sanctuary of your being. It's a slowing down, a turning inward with curiosity to listen to the quiet wisdom beneath doubt and distraction.

You are not here to fix or become someone else.
You are here to remember your wholeness, worth,
and deep connection to your own truth.
Your authentic voice—perhaps soft or buried at first—
holds the keys to your freedom.

Trusting that voice sparks your unique journey of self-discovery, inviting you to honor what resonates and to protect your peace with boundaries. Your path needs no approval but your own.

Some days you'll feel clear and connected; other days, uncertain and lost. This too is part of coming home. Each step brings you back to your center, where you move through life with quiet confidence, guided by your inner compass.

This journey began with a longing to know yourself. And now you see—you were never lost. You've always carried the light within. You didn't need to become someone else; you just needed to remember.

There is more to explore, unlearn, and awaken to. But now, you walk with awareness, intention, and soul.

You are the seeker and the wisdom.

The student and the teacher.

The mystery and the answer.

Welcome home.

Recognizing Your Own Wholeness

There is a quiet power in recognizing that you are already whole—not waiting to be fixed or patched, but fully embracing every part of yourself: light and shadow, strength and vulnerability. Wholeness isn't perfection; it's the fullness of your humanity and divinity intertwined.

When you see yourself this way, the need for external approval fades. You stop seeking to fill an invisible void because you realize the space was never empty—it was waiting for your acceptance all along. You are enough—not someday, not after more work or change, but *right now*.

Wholeness is not something to earn or piece together; it is your inherent state. To recognize your wholeness is to see yourself clearly and completely, including the parts that feel broken, unfinished, or uncertain. It's a gentle acceptance of your full human spectrum.

Often, we're conditioned to think wholeness means perfection—that if we fix enough or reach a milestone, we'll be "complete." But true wholeness doesn't erase imperfections; it welcomes them as vital threads in the fabric of who you are.

By recognizing your own wholeness, you step beyond the fragmented story of lack into a deeper truth: you are already enough. A complex, evolving being made of strengths, vulnerabilities, joys, and wounds—and all of it belongs.

This recognition frees you. It softens the pressure to prove yourself, chase approval, or constantly change. It invites you to rest in your own presence with compassion and honor your experiences, stories, and emotions as valid expressions of your unique journey.

Owning your wholeness means no longer seeking validation through external achievements or comparisons. Instead, you anchor in the deep knowing that your essence is already whole. From this grounded place, your life unfolds with greater ease, authenticity, and peace.

Releasing the Search

We often pour so much energy into searching—seeking meaning, purpose, validation, or peace—outside ourselves. It's easy to believe the next book, teacher, or experience will finally bring the clarity we crave. But what if the search itself is a sacred invitation to turn inward?

Releasing the search means letting go of the frantic chase for something "out there" and gently redirecting your attention back home. It's trusting that your seeking reflects a deeper longing to reconnect with your true self. You don't need to find something new—you need to remember what's already yours.

The quest for self-discovery often feels like a relentless outward journey—a pursuit of answers, validation, or a "better" version of yourself just beyond reach. But what if that very search is what keeps you from the peace and clarity you seek?

Releasing the search isn't giving up or settling. It's releasing the exhausting belief that fulfillment depends on acquiring more knowledge, approval, or proof. Instead, it's turning inward and recognizing the answers have been within you all along.

This release is an act of radical trust. It invites you to stop grasping and striving, and simply be present where you are now. To rest in the quiet knowing beneath the noise— the stillness that holds you steady amid uncertainty.

When you release the search, you free yourself from the pressure to perform or fit into someone else's mold of success or enlightenment. You give yourself permission to be imperfect, to grow at your own pace, and to trust your unique path.

This doesn't mean you stop evolving or learning. It means you stop searching as if something is missing and start living as if you are already whole. The search softens into curiosity, and curiosity blooms into presence.

In releasing the search, you create space for genuine connection—with yourself, others, and life unfolding as it is. You open your heart to receive rather than chase, to trust rather than doubt, and simply to be exactly as you are.

The Illusion of Separation

Much of our suffering arises from the feeling that we are separate—from our intuition, from others, and even from our own hearts. This sense of division stirs longing and doubt, as if something vital is missing. But beneath this illusion lies a deeper truth: you are not separate from your soul or the universe's flow.

As the walls of separation begin to dissolve, you feel a natural unity with yourself and life. This awareness creates space for compassion, trust, and belonging—both to yourself and the world around you.

One of the greatest barriers to truly knowing ourselves is the story of separation—the belief that we are isolated islands, apart from others, the world, and even our deeper selves. This illusion paints us as disconnected and alone in our struggles and triumphs.

Yet this sense of separation is just that—an illusion. Born from fear, conditioning, and the mind's need to control, it obscures the truth that we are deeply interconnected beings, woven into a vast web of life and spirit that unites us all.

When you see through this illusion, the rigid boundaries begin to soften. The parts of yourself you've hidden or denied become reflections of the whole. The "other" — the people, nature, and experiences you encounter — mirrors your inner landscape.

This recognition is freeing. It invites you to embrace belonging — not by fitting a mold, but as part of an interconnected flow that transcends individuality. Your joys, pains, and growth ripple outward and back in ways beyond your full understanding.

Understanding this interconnectedness dissolves loneliness, alienation, and disconnection. It nurtures compassion for yourself and others, reminding you we are all on this journey together, each carrying our own challenges and gifts.

The illusion of separation may keep you searching for wholeness "out there," but the truth is the thread connecting you to everything is already within. To know yourself fully is to recognize your place in the vast, intricate dance of existence — a dance that is never truly solitary.

Trusting Your Inner Wisdom

Your inner wisdom is a quiet, steady light that shines continuously, even when the world around you feels loud and confusing. It lives within your body, your emotions, and your intuition — a voice whispering truths your mind often struggles to express.

Learning to trust this inner guidance is a sacred practice. It means listening deeply—beyond fear, doubt, and the urge to please others—and honoring the truths that arise from your own experience. Your intuition is not a fleeting feeling; it is your soul's compass, always pointing you home.

Deep within you lies a wellspring of wisdom—a calm, steady presence that knows your truth beyond words or logic. This inner wisdom is your most authentic guide, patiently waiting for you to listen and trust.

Yet trusting this voice can feel daunting. For so long, many of us have sought answers outside ourselves—validation from others, advice from experts, or certainty in external achievements. But no matter how much we gather from the outside, the most profound truths already reside within.

Trusting your inner wisdom means tuning into the subtle knowing that rises in your body, heart, or mind. It is the gentle nudge or calm pause that steers you away from what no longer serves and toward what feels alive and true.
This trust is nurtured through presence and patience. It calls for slowing down, creating space for reflection, and quieting the noise of doubt and fear. Sometimes it speaks in whispers— through dreams, intuitive feelings, or moments of clarity. Other times, it emerges as a deep, unwavering certainty.

When you choose to trust your inner wisdom, you reclaim

your sovereignty. You step out of the shadows of others' expectations and begin to walk a path uniquely your own. This doesn't mean the path is always clear or easy— but it means you have a compass to guide you through uncertainty with resilience and grace.

Learning to trust yourself is a revolutionary act of self-love and empowerment. It invites you to honor your experiences, embrace your imperfections, and believe in your capacity to navigate life's unfolding journey.

Remember: your inner wisdom is not a distant goal to reach but a constant companion to welcome home. The more you listen, the stronger that voice becomes—and the more fully you can live as the person you already are.

The Power of Presence

Presence is the doorway to truly knowing yourself. When you bring your attention fully into the here and now, you step out of the restless seeking mind and into the spaciousness of simply being. In presence, the need to prove, perform, or fix gently dissolves. It is in the quiet of the moment that your true self reveals itself—whole, vibrant, and unshakable.

Presence invites you to experience life as it unfolds, grounded in your authentic knowing, free from the weight of past stories or future worries.

Presence is the art of deeply inhabiting each moment—
with openness, curiosity, and without distraction. When you
cultivate presence, you shift from living on autopilot or being
pulled by past regrets and future anxieties, toward embracing
the richness of what is here and now.

This presence isn't about forcing stillness or emptying your
mind. Rather, it's about showing up for yourself with gentle
awareness—welcoming whatever arises inside and around you
without judgment. It's a practice of tuning into the subtle
rhythms of your breath, the sensations in your body, and the
feelings coloring your experience.

The power of presence lies in its ability to anchor you in your
own truth. When you are fully present, you become attuned to
your inner voice, values, and needs. You begin to notice when
you stray from alignment—and can course-correct with
kindness instead of criticism.

Presence also gifts you freedom to experience life more
vividly—the colors grow brighter, conversations deepen, and
simple moments like a breath or a glance hold greater meaning.
This awakened way of being helps you step away from
distractions that pull you from your authentic self and
reconnect with what matters most.

Practicing presence is a radical act of self-respect. It says to
yourself: I am worthy of my own attention. I am here to witness

my life fully and without reservation.

The more you nurture presence, the more your inner authority and wisdom guide you with clarity. You learn to respond to life's challenges from a grounded place, rather than reacting out of fear or habit.

Presence is not a destination—it is a living, breathing practice that invites you to return again and again to the sanctuary within. It is where you meet the person you've been seeking all along.

Embracing the Journey Without Judgment

Remember, knowing yourself is not a race or a destination with a finish line. It's an ongoing, ever-evolving journey, full of growth, setbacks, doubts, and breakthroughs.

It's okay to stumble or feel lost sometimes.
These moments aren't failures—they are part of the unfolding.

Embrace yourself with kindness and curiosity as you navigate this path. Celebrate your courage to keep returning, again and again, to the truth within you. You are both the student and the teacher of your own life, and every step you take shines as a testament to your growing light.

The path to truly knowing yourself is not a straight line or a perfect script. It's a winding, often messy journey filled with twists, setbacks, and breakthroughs. Embracing this journey without judgment means giving yourself permission to be human—to stumble, to question, to rest, and to grow at your own pace.

When you release the need to measure your progress by others' standards or by a fixed idea of what "enlightenment" looks like, you create space for genuine transformation. You allow your experience to unfold naturally, honoring where you are right now instead of rushing toward where you think you should be.

This compassionate stance toward yourself invites freedom. It softens the inner critic and invites curiosity instead—curiosity about what your challenges reveal, what your joys teach, and how every step, even the difficult ones, contributes to your unfolding story.

Judgment often stems from fear—
fear of not being enough, of failure, or of uncertainty.
But when you embrace your journey without judgment,
you step into a deeper trust:
trust in your own resilience,
trust in your inner wisdom, and
trust in life's unfolding as it is meant to be.

Remember, you already are who you've been seeking. Every experience, every moment, is part of coming home to that truth. When you walk your path with kindness and openness, you honor the sacredness of your own becoming.

Let this be your ongoing invitation —
to show up for yourself with gentle acceptance,
to celebrate the progress you've made, and
to welcome all that you are becoming, exactly as you are.

The Path You Walk Is Your Own

As we close this chapter of your journey through these pages, remember—what you've discovered here is only a part of a much larger, unfolding story. This is not the end. In many ways, it is where your true journey begins. The work of knowing yourself, trusting your inner wisdom, and walking your own path has only just begun.

Carry with you what resonates, what stirs your soul, and gently release what doesn't. You alone hold the power to discern what fits your truth and what does not. You are the steward of your own growth and the author of your unfolding story.

As you continue to explore and evolve, know that this book is not a prescription, but a mirror—reflecting the wisdom that already lives within you, inviting you to remember. You are never alone on this path. You are woven into the infinite web of wisdom that stretches across time, space, and beyond.

Trust your path. Trust your knowing. The answers you seek have always been with you. All that remains is to listen, to feel, and to move forward from that deep, quiet place within.

And when doubt arises, when the road feels steep or uncertain, remember this: you are stronger than you realize. You carry within you a wellspring of resilience, courage, and light. Keep walking, keep trusting, and know that every step you take is a powerful act of becoming—brave, authentic, and uniquely you.

The journey is yours. Embrace it fully.

The Unfolding of the Journey

Your journey is a deeply personal and ongoing process. It won't look like anyone else's—and that's as it should be. There is no fixed map or step-by-step guide, only the choices and moments that arise for you.

That's what makes this journey meaningful: discovering what is truly yours to experience. There's no need to rush or to reach a specific endpoint. Each step you take is important, and every breath reminds you that you are already complete.

You may face times of doubt, confusion, or uncertainty about your path. These moments are natural. Let them pass without judgment. Underneath those feelings, your truth remains steady. When things feel unclear, come back to yourself. You have the ability to guide yourself forward.

You are not lost—you are uncovering the many parts of who you are. This work of self-discovery never really ends, and it changes as you grow. It's not about finding perfect answers but about learning to listen to what feels right for you.

When you take a good look at yourself, trust what you find. Trust the feelings, thoughts, and insights that come up. Know that you are moving forward with wisdom that comes from within and that will continue to grow.

Self-knowledge is a lifelong journey. As long as you keep exploring, you will continue to learn — step by step, moment by moment.

Thank you for sharing this part of the journey with me. Now the path is yours. Walk it with confidence, patience, and the understanding that you already have everything you need inside you.

About the Author

Kea Rivers is a writer and spiritual seeker who understands how deeply our inner selves are reflected in the people and experiences around us. Through years of personal growth and exploration, she has learned to recognize relationships and challenges as mirrors that invite us to remember who we truly are beneath the surface. Rooted in the belief that we are spiritual beings having a human experience, Kea offers a gentle, insightful guide to help readers embrace their journey of remembering and becoming. *Becoming Who You Already Are: A Journey of Self-Discovery and Spiritual Remembering* is a heartfelt invitation for seekers to reclaim their truth—truth that is not imposed, but felt, remembered, and reclaimed through inner knowing. Join her in this journey of self-discovery and spiritual remembering. Together, uncover the truth that has always lived within you.

WORKS:

- *Mirror Mirror, Seeing Pass the Reflection*